Advanced C:
Techniques and Applications

Gerald E. Sobelman

David E. Krekelberg

Que Corporation
Indianapolis, Indiana

Library of Congress Catalog No.: 85-60694
ISBN 0-88022-162-3

Editorial Director

David F. Noble, Ph.D.

Editors

Jeannine Freudenberger, M.A.
Katherine S. Ewing
Kathie-Jo Arnoff

Technical Editor

Chris DeVoney

88 87 86 85   8 7 6 5 4 3 2 1

Interpretation of the printing code: the rightmost double-digit number is the year of the book's printing; the rightmost single-digit
number, the number of the book's printing. For example, a printing
code of 85-4 shows that the fourth printing of the book occurred
in 1985.

Dedication

To Joanne
—G.E.S.

To my parents
—D.E.K.

About the Authors

Gerald E. Sobelman

Gerald E. Sobelman is a senior technical consultant at Control Data Corporation. He received a Ph.D. in physics from Harvard University and has been involved in the development of integrated circuits for five years. Dr. Sobelman has had more than 10 years of computer programming experience. He has published nine technical papers and has given presentations at several major technical conferences.

David E. Krekelberg

David E. Krekelberg is a computer-aided design research engineer at Control Data Corporation. He received a B.S.E.E. degree from the University of Minnesota Institute of Technology in 1982. At age 24, Mr. Krekelberg has more than 10 years of programming experience and has held software design positions at Sperry Corporation and Control Data Corporation. Mr. Krekelberg's work on CAD tool design and development has been published in the proceedings of several major technical conferences.

Table of Contents

7   Application Graphics

8   Advanced User Interfaces: Concepts

9   Advanced User Interfaces: The System

Appendix A

Appendix B

Appendix C

Appendix D

Index

Preface

This book is an excursion into the world of advanced programming in the C language. The book is written for several groups of programmers: first, those who have a basic knowledge of C and wish to extend their understanding of the language; second, programmers of C or of other languages who want to enhance their programming skills; and finally, programmers who are interested in building state-of-the-art applications, particularly applications involving graphics or advanced user interfaces.

The book is divided into three sections. The first part (chapters 1-4) deals with several advanced aspects of the C language itself, including techniques for designing large programs, the use of dynamic (updated) memory allocation, construction of user-defined data types, and the use of functions. Top-down design, information hiding, and the use of multiple source files are described. Pointers are emphasized throughout the book, especially in the descriptions of dynamic memory allocation and complex data types. In the chapter about functions, the stress is on two advanced topics: recursion and pointers to functions.

The second part of the book (chapters 5-6) examines in detail several techniques for constructing linked lists and trees. These techniques are presented in general formats so that the programmer can store and manipulate different types of elements. Various ways of extending the basic data structures are also discussed.

In the third part of the book (Chapters 7-9 and Appendixes A, B, and C), these ideas and techniques are illustrated through the construction of two related function libraries. The first function library (Appendix A) provides a set of routines by which applications programmers can generate and control complex graphics operations. Chapter 7 explains the basic concepts of the code presented in Appendix A. The second library (Appendix B) builds on the first. With the second library, programmers can implement an advanced user interface including multiple menus and windows. Chapter 9 explains the basic concepts of the code presented in Appendix B. Screen images derived from the code in Appendix B are in Appendix C.

The code that appears in Appendix A and B of this book is available from the Que Corporation on disk. To order, use the form in the back of the book.

We would like to thank Pegg Kennedy and Chris DeVoney of Que for their encouragement and assistance throughout the course of this project.

Gerald E. Sobelman
David E. Krekelberg

Minneapolis, Minnesota
1985

Trademark Acknowledgements

Que Corporation has made every attempt to supply trademark information about company names, products, and services mentioned in this book. Any trademarks indicated below were derived from various sources. Que Corporation cannot attest to the accuracy of this information.

UNIX is a trademark of Bell Laboratories, Inc.

1

Programming Style

Programming languages are tools for solving problems. The steps for solving a complex programming problem can be expressed in general terms, but to implement the solution on a computer, a specific programming language is required. Every language has special characteristics that dictate the style of coding necessary to achieve good results. As the size and complexity of the program increases, stylistic considerations become more important to the success of a programming project.

This chapter presents several methods for solving complex programming problems in the C language. In particular, the text introduces techniques for dividing large tasks into sets of functions and smaller files so that the programs run efficiently and are easily portable among different C environments.

Program Structure

C is an ideal language for the design and implementation of complex programming projects. This capability is due largely to the great flexibility provided by the proper use of functions. The language lends itself naturally to a top-down method of design, in which large and complex problems are broken down into successively smaller pieces. To use this technique, you begin by identifying the overall flow of control and the principal tasks. Then you can easily write a C pseudocode (a kind of structured English) description of the high-level design. In writing your descriptions, you assume that a function exists to perform each major task. Next, you examine the individual high-level functions and divide each function into a set of simpler ones. This refinement process can be con-

tinued until you reach a stage where you can write straight C code
to perform each required action.

Block Structure

An important difference between C and other modern programming languages (such as Pascal) is seen in C's concept of block
structure. In other languages, a complex function consists of a
package of smaller functions bundled together to form a single
larger unit. C treats all functions as separate entities. The set of
functions assembled to solve a particular programming problem
can be thought of as a collection of "tools" used to perform the job
at hand. With C you actually have a "toolbox" of functions that are
applicable to many programming projects.

This concept is best illustrated by an example. Suppose you want
to write a program that plays a board game with a user. Alternate
moves are made by each "player" until one side wins. At the highest level, the computer and the human player exchange a series of
moves; so you may start by writing pseudocode that describes the
main stages of the program. The statements of the pseudocode
can be easily translated into function calls. In this case, the main
function can be sketched as follows:

```
initialize game flags
initialize display
while the game is still on
    {
    if it's the computer's move
        {
        determine the next move
        update the display
        set flags according to result
        }
    else
        {
        wait for move to be entered
        check legality
        update the display
        set flags according to result
        }
    }
```

You should note several important points about the pseudocode. First, for every statement dictating some sort of action, you must create a function to perform that task. For this reason, the statements in the preceding pseudocode *initialize game flags, initialize display, determine the next move,* and so on, are candidates for high-level functions. Second, the control structures *while, if,* and *else* map directly into the corresponding C constructs. Finally, status phrases such as *the game is still on* and *it's the computer's move* translate into integer variables used to hold information about the current state of the game. These variables are used by the control structures to make decisions.

Most of these high-level functions are not simple enough to translate directly into C code, and the functions themselves must be broken down into smaller functions. For instance, consider the move generation function, which may be pseudocoded as follows:

```
find all legal moves
for all such moves
    {
    evaluate position
    if best move so far
        update selected move
    {
return selected move
```

This function follows the same pattern as the first one. Clearly, *find all legal moves* and *evaluate position* are themselves complex functions that can be further broken down. On the other hand, *update selected move* is probably simple enough to be coded directly in C. By following this procedure through to its conclusion, you can develop a full working program.

Whether you are writing pseudocode or actual C code, you must consider indentation and the location of braces in order to develop readable programs. C programs can easily be logically correct and completely unreadable. Several styles of arranging the text on the page are available. These styles ensure that the resulting code is easily understandable. The coding style used in this book is one that looks natural and clean. The important point, though, is for you to choose and stick to a style that suits you.

Variable Names
in Block Structure

The concept of block structure in C is evident in the scope of variable names. *Block* means the code between any matching pair of left and right braces. A block may be an entire function or a set of actions following a control structure like while, if, or else. You can define variables that are local to any specific block. For example, you frequently need a temporary variable to count some range of values. Access to this variable is probably not needed in other parts of the program. Therefore, defining the variable so that it is known only within the set of statements in which it is active makes sense. In the following code fragment, the variables items and min are defined outside the block, but the variable i, which is needed only within the block, is defined inside the block. The local version of the variable i does not interfere with another variable named i that may occur in the enclosing block or in a separate block.

```
int items, min;

/* set items and min to some values */
items = 3;
min   = 1;

        . . .


/* the block */
if (items > min)
    {
    /* define i to be local to this block */
    int i;

    /* begin loop that uses the local i as a counter */
    for (i = 0; i < items; ++i)
        {
        /* statements that will  be executed "items" times */


            . . .


        }
    }
```

The variables that have been discussed are called *automatic variables*. For these variables, storage is allocated at the entry to a block and deallocated at the exit from the block. No memory of previous values is retained on succeeding passes through the block. Before these variables are initialized, their values are unpredictable. You can override this default condition through the use of the static facility. A variable that is defined as *internal static* is allocated storage at the beginning of program execution and that storage is not deallocated until the program has terminated. This facility, then, provides a means for permanent private storage.

External variables are defined outside any block (and therefore outside any function) and are available for use within groups of functions. Function names are considered external and so are visible inside other functions. Controlling the extent of this visibility is important.

Separate Compilation and Information Hiding

C programs can be partitioned into several files. A good rule of thumb is to put logically related functions in the same file. Each file can be compiled independently and linked to other compiled files so that individual pieces of a large program can be debugged efficiently. If a compilation error is found, only a small portion of the program needs to be recompiled, and the edit-compile process can proceed rapidly. In addition, small *driver programs* that test the functions contained within a single file can be written. In this way, many run-time bugs can be fixed quickly on a file-by-file basis.

In addition to increasing efficiency, the careful use of separate files can be used to hide implementation details. This practice not only simplifies and modularizes the total program but also prevents the unintended overlap of variable or function names that may occur in a large program, especially if more than one person is involved in program design.

In a discussion of the visibility, or scope, of names in C, the definition of an external variable or a function must be distinguished from the variable's or function's declaration. An external element can be defined only once. In addition to specifying type information, the definition allocates storage and may also set initial values. An external name is visible in the file in which the name is defined from the point of definition until the end of the file. If the variable or function name is needed at an earlier position in that file or in another file, the name can be declared with the `extern` keyword. This declaration does not allocate storage but merely reserves a slot in the compiler's global name table so that the linker can tie together all the references to the common name. As an example, consider the following three files and their contents:

In file main.c

```
int     count = Ø, up, down;
double  x, y, z;

char    f1(num_1)
int     num_1;
{

    . . .

}

double  f2(num_2)
int     num_2;
{

    . . .

}
```

In file part1.c

```
extern  int     count;
extern  char    f1();

    . . .
```

In file part2.c

```
extern  int     count, up, down;
extern  double  x, y, f2();

    . . .
```

In this example, the variable `count` is available for use in all three files, but `up`, `down`, `x`, `y`, and the function `f2` are known only in the files main.c and part2.c. The function f1 is restricted to main.c and part1.c. In file part1.c, the keyword extern in the declaration of the function f1 is optional because files are extern by default. The same is true of the declaration of f2 in file part2.c.

Information hiding is accomplished through the use of the external static storage class. If an external variable or function is defined with the static prefix, the variable can be accessed only within that file. Thus, functions and external variables can be shared throughout a file and yet be totally unknowable in any other file. Information hiding is quite useful for implementing utility or library routines. In these situations, only the means of accessing the routine is important, and the details of implementation are properly hidden from the user. Consider the following example:

In file util.c

```
static   int      p, q;
static   double  r, s;

static   int f1(a, b)
int      a, b;
{

...

}


static   int f2(a, b, c)
char     a, b, c;
{

...

}


char     utility(x, y, z)
int      x, y, z;
{

...

}
```

The function utility can make calls to functions f1 and f2, and all three can read and write to the external variables p, q, r, and s. However, only the utility function itself can be seen from another file. Therefore, if the file user.c contains the declaration

```
extern  char    utility();
```

at the beginning of the file, functions within that file can gain access to utility through a call like

```
letter = utility(i,  j,  k);
```

Header Files

Logically connected groups of constants and data types that are used in different parts of a large program should be collected in a single file (known as a header file) and simply copied (by means of the #include facility) into the files that require the use of those elements. Another good general programming practice is to avoid *hard coding* (specifying explicitly) any numerical constants. Instead, define a suitable name for the constant and refer to that name when the value is needed. This practice promotes the generality of the code and provides easier debugging and maintenance.

C provides a technique that easily implements this type of program organization. The #define facility replaces a name with a character string throughout a file from the line of the name's definition until the end of the file. The replacement is done in a prepass by the compiler before any syntactic or semantic analysis is performed.

To illustrate these ideas, consider the situation in which you must specify a class of elements. Normally, in these cases, both the total number of elements in the category and a numerical code for each element are specified. For example, in a graphics application, your program may use a set of eight colors. A header file called colors.h can be created to contain the definitions of the colors.

```
#define COLORS  8    /* total number of colors */
#define BLACK   0
#define RED     1
#define GREEN   2
#define BLUE    3
#define CYAN    4
#define YELLOW  5
#define MAGENTA 6
#define WHITE   7
```

This file can be included in the appropriate files by the statement

```
#include "colors.h"
```

External Variables

Header files are also convenient for declaring external variables and defining structure types. If a set of variables is to be shared by different files, the variables are defined only once, typically in the file containing the main routine. Then, a set of corresponding extern declarations can be assembled in a separate file called globals.h. Any file can access the set of external variables by adding the following statement to the top of the file:

```
#include "globals.h"
```

Structure Types

Similarly, if a group of data types is needed in several files, the entire set of structure type definitions should be put into a single file called types.h. (Structures and type definitions are discussed in detail in Chapter 3.) Any file can then make use of this data type information by the addition of the simple statement

```
#include "types.h"
```

Of course, if your program uses several different classes of variables and/or types, the natural organization is to separate the items into different header files according to class and #include only the classes needed for each file. In most applications, a little careful forethought about the overall design of the program leads to a natural collection of files for that problem.

Macros with Arguments

Another powerful feature of C is the capability of defining macros with arguments. This facility permits simple functions to be expressed as macros, thereby eliminating the overhead (parameter passing) associated with making function calls. A single macro also can be used with arguments of different data types and so behave as a generic procedure. This convenient feature improves program readability and execution time.

As an example, study the following macro, which computes the sum of the squares of its arguments:

```
/* sum of squares */
#define SOS(x, y) ((x) * (x) + (y) * (y))
```

If your code requires the repeated computation of the sum of the squares of two numbers, using this macro instead of an analogous function decreases execution time. A function call and subsequent return involves a certain amount of overhead; but with the macro, the compiler performs a direct, in-line substitution of code. Specifically, on its prepass, the compiler replaces the statement

```
e = SOS(a + b, c + d);
```

with

```
e = ((a + b) * (a + b) + (c + d) * (c + d));
```

This example demonstrates clearly that you must include enough sets of parentheses to ensure that the macro's operations are carried out in the desired order for any set of arguments. As a matter of safety, also enclose the entire macro definition in parentheses, as in the preceding example. These parentheses guarantee the correct precedence of operations even when the macro is used as an element in a complex expression. Note also that no type information is contained in the macro. The macro merely substitutes variable names and thereby types, according to each specific instance in which the macro is used. Thus, although macros look like functions, macros compile and therefore act quite differently.

Portability and Hardware Independence

During the coding phase of a large project, you should keep portability considerations constantly in mind. Even though you may think that a particular program will always be compiled with a certain compiler and be run only on a given machine, circumstances may change. When new compilers and faster machines appear, a "dedicated application program" is suddenly a candidate for transfer to a new environment. In other cases, code developed to run on microcomputers may be found to be suitable for porting to mainframes. In any event, allowing for any future transfer of code to new systems is always wise.

Fortunately, C programs are, for the most part, easily transportable. Because of the almost universal acceptance of the standard set forth in Appendix A of the classic book, *The C Programming Language* by B. W. Kernighan and D. M. Ritchie,[1] agreement on the precise definition of the language is widespread. As a general rule, you should be wary of using any nonstandard enhancements of a particular compiler. Any marginal gain in code compactness or efficiency may be more than offset by future transportability problems.

The consideration of portability also applies to any piece of code that is specific to a piece of hardware. This limitation typically occurs in input or output routines and may involve such details as the choice of color or monochrome for the display type, the number of horizontal and vertical lines or pixels available, the use of specially defined keys, or the properties of a positioning device like a mouse.

Any routines of this kind should be written using a layered approach, with generic functions that make calls to other hardware-specific functions. As shown in the diagram in figure 1.1, the application routines make calls to a set of interface functions that are to perform the harware-specific tasks. Each of these interface functions would be implemented using the primitives of the target machine. In this way, the code contained in the application routines will be fixed; only the set of interface routines needs to be changed for a new environment.

All these nonportable hardware-specific functions should be collected in a single file, which is compiled separately. The *hooks* (ways of interfacing) into the routines within this file should be simple and well defined. If this procedure is followed, moving the program to a different hardware environment involves making changes to the code in only this single file. All the routines involving I/O presented in this book are constructed in this manner.

A related situation is the case in which a single compiled block of code is to be run on a specified processor with varying peripherals at different times. For instance, in a microcomputer environment, sometimes a color display screen is available, but at other times or installations, only a monochrome display is attached. For these situations, you create a separate file that contains a small routine which determines the current system configuration. At the begin-

---

[1] B. W. Kernighan and D. M. Ritchie, *The C Programming Language* (Englewood Cliffs, N.J.: Prentice-Hall, Inc., 1978), Appendix A.

ning of program execution, this routine "makes inquiries" to the hardware and/or the user to determine what types of peripherals are available. The routine then sets the corresponding program variables. Having set the variables, the program can proceed without encountering any unanticipated situations.

In summary, you should take a little extra effort to organize a program so that the design, debugging, maintenance, and portability are enhanced. C is an extremely expressive and powerful language for developing large programs. By following the guidelines set forth in this chapter, you can build systems of amazing complexity and capability.

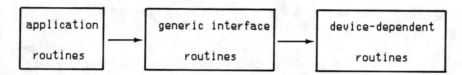

Fig. 1.1. Layered approach for hardware-specific functions.

2
Pointers and Dynamic Memory Allocation

Pointers give C much of its distinctive personality. Although beginning programmers are sometimes reluctant to use this feature of the language, most advanced applications programs require extensive use of pointers. They provide the flexibility required for expressing complex interrelationships of data and can also considerably improve the run-time performance of many programs.

However, with increased power comes added responsibility. The improper use of pointers causes countless difficulties. In fact, in some cases a bad pointed value can cause an inadvertent loss of other important data.

This chapter discusses many subtleties involved in the use of pointers. Particular attention is given to the problem of memory allocation. When you are working with pointers, the essential considerations are to keep in mind precisely what elements are being manipulated in expressions and to know whether adequate storage has been allocated for the intended operation.

Pointers and Arrays

Pointers and arrays are closely related features in C. Both are used to control access to groups of elements having a common type. However, an array is effective only when the precise number of elements is known at compile time so that the correct storage can be allocated. If the number of elements cannot be known until run time, an array implementation either allocates too much space and wastes resources or, worse, does not allocate enough space and thereby creates a "disaster waiting to happen."

Pointers

In most sophisticated applications, the exact number of elements in the different types of data structures is not known at compile time. Because the number varies with the program's actions, allocating individual pieces of storage as needed is most sensible. In this way, you always have the correct amount of storage at any given moment of program execution. Pointers can be used effectively in situations where the number of elements in the data structures changes as the program is running.

A pointer is simply the location, or address, where data is stored. The pointer "points" to the place where information is to be found. Two C operators, & and *, give the programmer access to pointers. For the first operator, the proper usage is

```
&( . . . )
```

This statement can be read as "the address of (. . .)", and the (. . .) means some variable or expression. The second operator,

```
*( . . . )
```

stands for "the contents of (. . .)". Here, (. . .) represents an address where information has been stored.

In definitions and declarations, the * operator is also used to indicate that certain variables or functions are pointers. For example, consider the following definitions:

```
float *x, *f();
```

This statement means, literally, that the quantities *x and *f() are elements of type float. Thus, x must be a pointer to a variable of type float because applying the contents-of operator yields an object of type float. Similarly, the contents of the value returned by the function f is of type float, so f itself must return a pointer to an element of type float.

Notations of Pointers and Arrays

C has a convenient shorthand notation that is useful in array and pointer manipulations. An array name itself represents the base

address for a contiguous block of storage that holds the array contents. That is, the name of an array is a synonym for the address of
the zero element of that array. For example, if ary[N] is defined to
be an array of N integers, &ary[0] can be denoted simply by ary.
Because array elements are stored sequentially in the tightest possible space (allowing for any subtleties involving byte and word
boundaries), just enough space is allocated to hold each element's
data without any overlap. Thus, the i element of an array is located
at an address that is the sum of the base address for the array (ary)
plus i times the space required for each unit of array element storage. The shorthand notation for &ary[i] is written as ary+i. Note
that this notation properly reduces to simply ary when i is zero.
This relationship can also be looked at from the complementary
point of view. The contents stored in the i element of ary, which in
array language is written as ary[i], can be expressed in pointer
notation as *(ary+i).

The plus signs in all these expressions are simply mnemonics and
do not necessarily mean simple addition. The addition is automatically scaled by the size in bytes of the individual data items in
the array. Therefore, you need never be concerned about pointing
to an address in the middle of a block of storage, where the address does not correspond to a data value boundary.

These examples are special cases of address arithmetic in C. In
general, pointer variables can be incremented or decremented.
You can also assign to a pointer variable a pointer plus an integer
or a pointer minus an integer. In all cases, an appropriate scaling
of the operators is performed automatically by the compiler.

Two subtle points arise in the use of pointers and arrays. First, note
that array names are *pointer constants*. That is, when defined in a
program, an array name is assigned some address by the computer. This address is fixed and may not be changed by any program statement. Second, a programmer may choose to use either
the array or pointer notation in any given expression. The choice
is influenced by program readability considerations, not by the
terms of the original definition of the element. Internally, the compiler translates any square brackets used to indicate array elements into address arithmetic.

When you are deciding whether to define variables as arrays or
with pointers, keep in mind the question of exactly when storage
is allocated. For example, the definition

```
double x[NUM];
```

indicates that storage will be allocated for NUM elements of type double, and that the name x will hold the address of the zero element. On the other hand,

```
double *x;
```

indicates that the only storage allocated is for the pointer x itself. No space is reserved for any actual double-precision floating-point variables.

String Constants

One of the most common (and potentially confusing) examples of the use of pointers and arrays is that of string constants. Internally, strings are stored as arrays of characters. C uses the convention that the end of a string is flagged by the special character ' \0' . Thus, to store a string of length N, you need room for at least N + 1 characters. The confusion about string constants arises from trying to sort out exactly what data is being stored and referenced in various expressions.

A string constant consists of text appearing between quotation marks, as in

```
"This is a C string constant"
```

If a string constant appears in an expression, the compiler allocates just enough storage for the string (space for one more than the number of characters in the string) and sets a pointer to the starting address. Thus, if you have

```
char    *start;

. . .

start = "This is a C string constant";
```

the compiler allocates sufficient storage, puts the string in that area of memory, and assigns the address of the beginning of the string to the character pointer start. Then start[3], which is the same as *(start+3), is the fourth letter in the string, s. (Remember that the first element of a string is numbered zero.) Even though start was originally defined using pointer notation, start[i] makes good sense and can be used if desired.

A related situation, however, is not so nicely behaved. Consider trying to do the same assignment using the string copy function, strcpy. This function, which is supplied as a standard part of most C environments, copies strings, character by character, from one place in memory to another. However, if you try to replace the previous assignment statement with the following innocent-looking statement

```
strcpy(start, "This is a C string constant");
```

you will probably be in real trouble. In this case, the compiler allocates storage for the text between the quotation marks and returns a pointer to the beginning of that storage area. However, the strcpy function "assumes" that adequate storage is reserved at the destination (the address given by the pointer start). Because you have done nothing to ensure that adequate storage is indeed available, you may end up wiping out whatever was contained in the memory locations following the address given by start. The string copy works but often destroys another part of the program.

Storage Allocators

When an array is defined, storage is automatically allocated by the compiler. When you are using pointers, however, you must allocate the storage. Two C standard library functions are provided for this purpose. These functions are malloc (memory allocate) and calloc (contiguous allocate). The malloc function allocates a single piece of storage space, and calloc allocates an entire set of storage locations through a single function call. In addition, calloc fills the total storage space with zeros, but malloc leaves the area uninitialized.

Using malloc

Consider first the simpler function, malloc. The function definition, supplied as part of the standard C environment, is

```
char        *malloc(size)
unsigned    size;
{
. . .
}
```

Two points about this definition are significant. First, the malloc function returns a character pointer. This fact may seem odd because this function is to be used for allocating space for any type of element, not just characters. Because all C functions must be formally defined to return a specific type of variable, a character pointer was chosen arbitrarily. However, the function properly allocates the required space in all situations. The potential mismatch of types is easily fixed with a simple cast operation. The use of such a cast, which assigns the returned pointer value to a variable of the proper type, is illustrated below. Second, notice that the argument of the function, `size`, indicates the amount of storage to be allocated. In practice, `size` is normally the value returned by the C `sizeof` operator. This operator, which determines the size in bytes required to store the operator's argument, can be used in two ways. You can either supply a literal C variable name or expression, or you can use a standard or user-defined variable type name. In the first case, you write

        `sizeof` expression

where *expression* is a valid C expression. In the second case, the proper format is

        `sizeof` (type name)

For example, if the variable n has been defined as an integer, `sizeof` n and `sizeof(int)` both return the number of bytes of storage required for an integer variable.

Using `calloc`

When using `calloc`, you need to supply two pieces of information: the number of elements and the size of the individual element. The `calloc` function is handy when you know that a number of contiguous storage locations will be needed at once. Alternatively, if you want storage for only one item but want the item initialized to zero, you may choose to use `calloc` with a number argument of one.

Dealing with Changing Storage Needs

You are now in a position to fix the `strcpy` problem posed in the previous section. Proceed as follows:

```
char *start, *cons, *calloc();
```

```
/* safe transfer of string constant */
cons = "This is a C string constant";
start = calloc(strlen(cons) + 1, sizeof(char));
strcpy(start, cons);
```

This fragment uses another standard C function, strlen, which returns the length of the function's argument string. First allocate sufficient memory to receive the string; only then can you safely copy the data.

As a second example, consider the situation when you require dynamic storage (allocated while the program is executing) for a single float variable. First, define a float pointer, then make a call to one of the storage allocation routines, as follows:

```
float *place;

place = (float *) malloc(sizeof(float));

/* alternative:
place = (float *) calloc(1, sizeof(float));
*/
```

The new usage here is the cast, (float *). Even though the malloc or calloc function senses that it must reserve storage for a float-sized element, the function still returns a character pointer. Because place is a float pointer, you can correct this mismatch by a cast operation that performs type coercion, the creation of a new variable having the desired type. The general format for a cast is

new variable = (type name) old variable;

In the previous example, the type name is float *, which is read as "float pointer."

Because this combination of storage allocation and type coercion occurs so frequently, macros are useful to implement these operations automatically. In particular, you may use

```
#define MALLOC(x)      ((x *) malloc(sizeof(x)))
#define CALLOC(n, x)   ((x *) calloc(n, sizeof(x)))
```

Then, the allocation can be written as

```
place = MALLOC(float);
```

or

```
place = CALLOC(1, float);
```

The macro names and the standard function names are not con-
fused because C recognizes the difference between uppercase
and lowercase characters. (In this book, macro names always are
defined as uppercase.)

Using NULL Pointers

Another C convention, which involves NULL pointers, is convenient.
A valid pointer value (that is, one which indicates an actual memory
address) cannot be zero. This fact provides a scheme for detecting
errors in requests for storage space. For example, you may have
requested more space than the operating system can provide. In
this case, the convention is to have malloc or calloc return a zero
value, a NULL pointer. However, other reasons relating to access
rights violations may also cause a value of NULL to be returned.
When you use these functions, you should include a check to see
that such an allocation error has not occurred. For instance, you
can write

```
if (place = MALLOC(float))
    {
    /* proceed with intended action */
    ...


    }
else
    {
    /* flag error condition */
    printf("Allocation error on call to malloc\n");
    exit(1);
    }
```

Note that this code fragment uses the C shorthand that a nonzero
value (that is, a valid address) in the if condition triggers the "true"
branch, and a zero value causes control to flow to the else clause.

Freeing Blocks of Memory

Just as storage can be allocated dynamically, you can also free
blocks of memory when they are no longer needed. This is accomplished by making calls to the C free function, which is supplied
in the standard C working environment. This function has the form,

```
free(location)
char    *location;
{
...
}
```

The character pointer location is an address that was returned to the program by an earlier invocation of malloc or calloc. Free returns to the operating system the block of storage that was given to the program by malloc or calloc. Note that the calls to free previously allocated blocks of storage can be made in any order, regardless of how the blocks were originally obtained.

Freeing can be important in programs that perform much dynamic memory allocation. Obviously, the amount of memory available to an application program is finite, and at some point you may receive a NULL pointer from a malloc or calloc call. Two different strategies are possible. You can free storage as soon as it is no longer needed by the program, or you can wait until a NULL pointer is returned. In the latter case, the normal sequence of events must be suspended while the program attempts to free some space. The request for memory must then be repeated.

Using realloc

One more allocation function is furnished with most C systems. This function, realloc, changes the size of a previously allocated area of memory. The form of the function is

```
char      *realloc(location, size)
char      *location;
unsigned  size;
{
          ...
}
```

This function changes the amount of memory allocated at the starting address location to the amount specified by the argument size. This new area may be larger or smaller than what was previously allocated. Note, however, that if the new size is larger than the old one, the operating system may have to move to an entirely different area of memory to accommodate the request. If this happens, the old space is automatically freed. Whether the data is moved or not, the realloc function returns a pointer to the beginning of the new memory area.

Complex Associations of Data

Pointers and arrays can be combined to implement more complex associations of data. A simple example is an array of pointers. In this case, a fixed number of elements point to dynamically sized items. For instance, consider the example of reading in and subsequently storing a fixed number of character strings. You can solve this problem by using an array of pointers, in which each array element is a character pointer to a variable-length name. Although the lengths of the names may vary, the number of pointers is fixed. This array of pointers can be defined as

```
char    *name[TOTAL];
```

Note carefully the precedence of operations. This statement defines an *array* of pointers, *not* a single pointer that points to an array. The compiler responds by allocating space to hold all the character pointers. When you point to specific names, you will have to allocate the correct additional space for each name.

In order to see how this data structure works, study the following program fragment, which reads in a fixed number of names and allocates adequate storage according to the length of each name:

```
/* standard library file */
#include <stdio.h>

/* program constants */
#define TOTAL   10       /* number of names */
#define MAX_LEN 50       /* maximum name length */

/* storage allocator */
#define CALLOC(n, x)    ((x *) calloc(n, sizeof(x)))

main()
 /* read in names and allocate storage in
        preparation for later manipulations */
{
        char    *name[TOTAL];           /* array of pointers to names */
        char    buffer[MAX_LEN + 1];    /* input buffer */
        int     i;
```

```
                     /* print directive to user */
                     printf("Enter %d names, one per line\n", TOTAL);

                     /* begin input loop */
                     for (i = 0; i < TOTAL; ++i)
                         {
                         /* define local variables */
                         char    c;
                         int     length = 0;

                         /* prompt and read a name */
                         printf("\nName #%d? ", i + 1);
                         while ((c = getchar()) != '\n')
                                 if (length < MAX_LEN)
                                     buffer[length++] = c;
                         /* "stringify" name just read */
                         buffer[length] = '\0';

                         /* allocate appropriate storage and copy into it */
                         name[i] = CALLOC(length, char);
                         strcpy(name[i], buffer);
                         }

                 /* continue processing */

                 ...

  }
```

In this fragment, all names are first read into a buffer with a length set to some "safe" value large enough to accommodate all names. (In this case, the value is 50 characters.) When an actual name is given to the program, the program will allocate just enough storage for the name and the C string termination character. Finally, the name is copied to its own storage area, and the next name is read into the buffer.

The alternative method is to use a two-dimensional array, but this practice wastes storage for two reasons. First, because of the "rectangular" nature of multidimensional arrays, the storage required for the longest name is also allocated for all the other names, including the very short ones. Second, because the longest name cannot be accurately predicted, you must choose a "safe" large number, a practice that wastes even more space.

Pointers supply the addresses of elements. The element pointed to also can be another address. Sometimes, to obtain the desired data, you may require two different addresses. The first pointer indicates where to find an item that itself is an address. The desired data value is found in the location specified by the second address.

This idea may seem strange at first, but you may have good reasons for arranging some program data this way. One reason is related to generality of code and a corresponding postponement of specific choices. This may be the case when you are dealing with some run-time data. Another reason has to do with execution speed and efficiency. Many times, instead of explicitly transferring large amounts of data between program segments, transferring pointers is more convenient. In complicated situations, you may need to transfer only a portion of a large data structure. In this case, pointers to pointers are invaluable.

Pointers to pointers, particularly in combination with structures and unions, form the basis of many useful data structures. For instance, consider again the previous example of reading in a series of names. In some situations, the number of names may not be known at compile time but will vary from run to run. In this case, an array of pointers to names would be wasteful or dangerously lacking in space. You have a situation with a variable number of elements, each of which is of variable size. In order to handle this effectively, you need a pair of pointers, one that points to the actual name and a corresponding pointer that points to the location where information about the next name can be found. This combination forms the basis for the linked-list data structure, which is discussed in detail in Chapter 5.

Another important application of pointers, which has not yet been mentioned, is function selection. During program execution, depending on the current state of the program, you may want to select from among several methods for carrying out a certain task. Alternatively, you may have a single task but many possible entities on which you want to operate by making a choice based on run-time data. This dynamic selection mechanism can be implemented in C by using pointers to functions. This important topic is presented in Chapter 4.

3

Structures, Unions,
and Fields

Structures and unions form the basis for constructing the combinations of data required for complex programming projects. Using structures and unions provides a means for associating groups of variables in ways that naturally express the underlying form of a problem. By constructing the program with structures and unions, the programmer, in effect, extends the language to suit the situation by defining customized data types.

Fields, although syntactically similar to structures and unions, have unique applications. Fields are useful in situations when the program must descend to the bit level and interface directly with the hardware. Fields provide a convenient way of communicating between the high-level realm of the applications programmer and the nuts and bolts of data buses and input/output ports.

This chapter reviews the techniques for defining and using structures, unions, and fields and lays the groundwork for the advanced data structures and applications presented in the latter parts of the book.

Structures

Structures provide a convenient method for grouping logically related items. In a sense, structures are generalizations of arrays. All the elements of an array, of course, must be of the same data type. However, the elements of a structure can consist of any combination of standard or user-defined data types. Structures can be nested; that is, structures can be elements in other structures. They can even be used recursively.

Structures can be used to create new data types. Variables can then be defined to be of these types and manipulated within programs. The general format for defining a structure is

```
struct struct-tag
    {

    variable-definitions

    } variable-list;
```

The optional *struct-tag* is used as a label for the new structure type. *Variable-definitions* means the set of definitions of the individual items that make up the structure, and *variable-list* is a list of the variables that are defined to be structures of this type.

This format is the most direct way of defining variables to be of a certain structure type; but for complex data structures and applications, the C typedef facility is more convenient and increases program readability. Using typedef, you associate a name with a new data type. Then variables can be defined to be of this type in the same way that ordinary variables are defined. The typedef statement is written as

```
    typedef struct  struct-tag  type-name;
```

In this statement, *struct-tag* is a previously defined structure label, and *type-name* is the name of the new data type. (By convention and for promotion of program readability, all type names used in this book end in _t.) Once the typedef statement has been placed in a program, a variable can be defined to be of that type by a statement of the form

```
  type-name  variable-list;
```

These principles are illustrated by the following simple structure definition:

```
    /* define new structure type, "program" */
    struct program
        {
        char   *name;
        int    num_lines, num_chars;
        double run_time;
        };
```

```
/* define new data type, "prog_t" */
typedef struct program prog_t;

/* define elements to be of this type */
prog_t  my_prog, ur_prog;
```

You can also define an array, each of whose elements is a structure of this type, as in

```
prog_t  prog[QTY];
```

QTY, of course, has been specified in some previous #define statement.

To give access to the individual components of a structure, C provides the dot notation. In general, in order to pick out a particular component of a structure, you use the following format:

```
structure_variable_name . structure_member_name
```

Specifically, you may have program statements such as

```
int       how_many;

   . . .


my_prog. name = "whiz_bang";
how_many = prog[3]. num_lines;
```

Note carefully how the combination of operators works in the second assignment. The operators [] and . are of equal precedence and evaluate from left to right. First, the brackets select the element 3 of the array, and then the dot selects the num_lines component of that structure.

Pointers to Structures

As with simple variables, structures may have to be created as a program's execution proceeds. Predefined arrays of structures waste storage or contain inadequate amounts of storage. Therefore, pointers to structures can be used to create flexible units of program memory. Pointers to structures also provide important facilities for working with functions.

Pointers to structures are created in the same way that pointers to simple variables are defined. Consider, for example, a structure of the program type defined above.

```
prog_t  *example;
```

This statement means that the variable `example` is a pointer to a structure of type `prog_t`. Note that the statement allocates storage only for the pointer itself, not for a structure to which the pointer points. Furthermore, as with all pointers, you may not use `example` in a program statement until the variable has been set to hold some address.

To allocate space dynamically for a structure to which `example` can point, you can use the previously defined macro

```
example = MALLOC(prog_t);
```

This macro allocates enough storage to store all the components of the structure and assigns the starting address for this storage to the variable `example`. To access a component of this newly allocated structure, you use the dot notation:

```
(*example).num_lines
```

The parentheses are necessary because the precedence of the structure member dot operator (.) is higher than that of the * operator. Fortunately, a convenient shorthand notation for this frequently used construction is

```
example->num_lines
```

The natural-looking symbol `->` is a minus sign followed by a right arrow (or "greater than" symbol), and this shorthand notation is equivalent to `(*example).num_lines`. Not only is this notation more convenient, but it is also more suggestive of the intended operation and thereby promotes program readability.

As with pointers to simpler elements like character strings, pointers to structures improve execution speed. If a structure is large, transferring pointers from one part of a program to another is faster than copying all the individual components of the structure. The larger the structure, the greater the gain in speed that can be achieved.

A major use for pointers to structures occurs in the interaction of structures with functions. In C, you cannot pass a complete structure to a function simply by using the structure's name in the function's parameter list. Of course, you can list each structure component in the parameter list, but this listing is tedious for complex structures. Similarly, you cannot return a complete structure from a function because you can return only a single component value. Pointers to structures, however, can be used to get around these limitations. You can pass, as a function argument, a pointer to a structure or have a function return a pointer to another structure. Consider the following example:

```
main()
{
    send_t  *inp_var;
    rcve_t  *out_var, *trans();

    . . .

    out_var = trans(inp_var);

    . . .

}

rcve_t  *trans(input)
send_t  *input;
{
    rcve_t  *output;

    . . .

    return(output);
}
```

In the example, send_t and rcve_t are structure types that have been defined previously, perhaps in a header file. Before you use inp_var in the call to the trans function, you must allocate storage for a structure of type send_t and assign values to the structure's components. You must do the same for the returned variable before you leave the function.

When you use pointers to structures as function arguments, you can gain two advantages. First, using pointers can serve simply as a convenience; you do not have to list each structure component in the argument list. Second, you can get around the "call by value" rule of C. That is, by sending the address of the data, you have the possibility of altering the original data from within a called function. When returning a pointer to a structure from a function, you achieve an advantage not otherwise available: the ability to return more than one variable from a function. All you need to do is define a new structure type whose components are the set of values that need to be returned. Each time the function is called, it returns a pointer that indicates where the data can be found. Thus, the C rule, which permits only a single value to be returned from a function and so looks like a limitation to programmers familiar with other languages, is not a restriction at all.

A useful programming convention involving pointers and structures is the class of functions that *instantiates* (allocates and initializes) storage for elements of a given data type. For example, consider a data type that specifies a rectangle.

```
struct rect_primitive
    {
    int left, bottom, right, top;
    };
typedef struct rect_primitive rect_t;
```

You can write a function that allocates storage to hold one rect_t element and initializes its components at the same time, as follows:

```
rect_t *inst_rect(l, b, r, t)   /* instantiate rectangle */
int l, b, r, t;
{
    rect_t  *box;

    if (box = MALLOC(rect_t))
        {
        /* storage allocated, initialize components */
        box->left   = l;
        box->bottom = b;
        box->right  = r;
        box->top    = t;
        }
    else
        {
        /* flag error condition */
        printf("Allocation error on call to inst_rect with
                parameters %d, %d, %d, %d\n", l, b, r, t);
        exit(1);
        }
    /* return starting address of initialized storage */
    return(box);
}
```

With this kind of function, an element of type `rect-t` can be allocated and initialized (instantiated) with a simple statement of the form

```
new_obj = inst_rect(x1, y1, x2, y2);
```

The variable `new_obj` has been defined to be a pointer to `rect_t`; and x1, y1, x2, and y2 have been defined as integers. Obviously, this method can be applied for instantiating elements of any given data type simply by writing a similar function for each case.

Structure Nesting

You can also make structures the elements in other larger structures. Nesting may be accomplished by placing structures inside of structures or by using pointers to structures as the elements. The latter approach promotes generic code and may allow faster data transfer.

Consider the following example:

```
struct part
    {
    int     number;
    char    *name;
    };
typedef struct part part_t;

struct tech
    {
    int     grade, salary, years;
    char    *name;
    };
typedef struct tech tech_t;

struct shop
    {
    part_t  a, b, c[ITEMS];
    tech_t  *lead, *team[MEMBERS];
    };
typedef struct shop shop_t;
```

In this case, `shop_t` is made up of instances of type `part_t` with pointers to elements of type `tech_t`. You can define more complex elements by using the simple statement

```
shop_t  *x,  y,  z;
```

This statement allocates space for x, a pointer to an element of type shop_t, and for two explicit variables of that type, y and z. Each variable contains storage for ITEMS + 2 structures of type part_t and for MEMBERS + 1 pointers to structures of type tech_t. In addition, each structure of type part_t contains storage space for an integer and a character pointer, and the tech_t structures contain storage for three integer variables and one character pointer. Clearly, although calculating the total amount of storage required for any given compound structure is normally straightforward, the calculation can, in practice, result in complex combinations of variable and address storage.

The rules for accessing components of complex structures are simple and easy to apply. With the appropriate combinations of the and -> symbols from left to right, you can arrive at the desired data item. Because these two symbols and the [] are of equal precedence and operate from left to right, no parentheses are required to proceed from a composite element inside to a composite element's individual components. For example, in the previous example, you could use any of the following:

```
x->a. number
```

```
x->lead->name
```

```
y. c[i]. number
```

When using these complex structures, you must keep in mind exactly what is being defined and the points at which storage is being allocated for the various pieces. Remember that if a structure contains pointers, allocating space for the structure does *not* allocate space for the elements that are pointed to by those pointers. This space must be allocated separately by appropriate calls to the macros MALLOC or CALLOC.

Finally, structures may contain components that are pointers to structures of the same type. At first, this idea might seem contradictory or ill-defined, but it is not. You *will* have problems if you attempt to place actual instances of a structure inside itself, but all that is being discussed here is using pointers to that element. Only an address can fill that structure component's slot. These recursive structure definitions are useful in many complex data types, such as lists and trees (which are discussed in chapters 5 and 6, respectively). This idea is illustrated in the following example:

```
struct self
    {
    int        x, y, z;
    struct self *p, *q, *r;
    };
typedef struct self self_t;

self_t  s, t, u;
```

In this example, the self_t variables s, t, and u each contain three integers and three pointers, and each pointer variable points to another self_t element.

Inside such a self-referential structure, you should not use the type name that is defined by a subsequent typedef statement. Instead use the structure tag. The type name is not known to the compiler until it has analyzed the C code down to the typedef statement, whereas the structure tag name is available before the compiler enters the structure. Some compilers may permit the use of the type name inside the structure, but others do not.

Unions

A union provides a way for different types of data to be stored in a common block of memory space. This feature is useful in situations where a program uses items that play logically similar roles but these items differ in their detailed forms. In these cases, referring to the items by a generic name is desirable. The compiler allocates sufficient space to hold the largest item in the union (if the items are of different sizes), but the programmer is responsible for keeping track of what is currently stored in the union.

A simple example is the following union definition:

```
union value
    {
    int     int_item;
    double  dbl_item;
    };
typedef union value value_t;
```

In order to keep track of what type of item is stored at any given time, define an associated integer variable and form a composite element, known as a *variant record*, as follows:

```
struct var_rec
    {
    int     type;
    value_t item;
    };
typedef struct var_rec var_rec_t;
```

In this case, you can use a series of #defines to encode the indicated type, as in

```
#define INT Ø
#define DBL 1
```

The rules for accessing the elements of a union are the same as the rules for accessing structures. For example, if you have the variables

```
var_rec_t   nbr, *ptr;
```

you can have

```
nmbr.type, nmbr.item.int_item
```

or

```
ptr->item.dbl_item
```

as possible union element selections.

Fields

In some programming applications, you must manipulate individual bits within certain registers or memory locations. This necessity arises in two different situations. First, memory space may be at a premium, and everything must be done to conserve storage. Second, you may need to interact with specific hardware, such as with an external-device driver routine. In the latter situation, certain bits of a word correspond to hardware-dependent features that need to be controlled bit by bit. C provides a data construct, called a *field*, that makes either situation easy to deal with.

As for the union, the syntax for a field is similar to that for a structure definition. For example, consider a situation in which you must keep track of the data corresponding to a parallel port in a microprocessor system. You will have

```
struct port
   {
   unsigned     bit_0 : 1;   /*         -         */
   unsigned     bit_1 : 1;   /*         -         */
   unsigned     bit_2 : 1;   /*         -         */
   unsigned     bit_3 : 1;   /*         -         */
   unsigned     bit_4 : 1;   /* low byte */
   unsigned     bit_5 : 1;   /*         -         */
   unsigned     bit_6 : 1;   /*         -         */
   unsigned     bit_7 : 1;   /*         -         */
   unsigned     hi_by : 8;   /* high byte */
   };
typedef struct port port_t;
```

The integer after the colon is the number of bits assigned to that variable. In this case, you have defined a new data type that is composed of eight one-bit variables (which correspond to the low-order byte of a sixteen-bit variable) and one eight-bit variable (representing the high byte of the same variable). Note that, according to standard usage, each variable is defined to be of type unsigned in order to emphasize the elementary bit nature of the underlying elements. Because all these quantities are highly machine dependent, the field definition properly belongs in a file separate from the rest of the applications program.

When the compiler encounters a field definition, the compiler allocates storage as if the field were one or more integer variables. The smallest number of integers required by the machine being compiled for are allocated. In the example, on a very small machine that has integers stored as eight-bit quantities, a variable of type port_t requires two integer variable positions. On the other hand, for machines where integers are sixteen bits or larger, a single integer location suffices.

Components of a field are accessed in exactly the same manner as ordinary structures. Therefore, if you define two variables as

```
port_t a_reg, *b_reg;
```

you can refer to individual components as, for example,

```
a_reg.bit_3, a_reg.hi_by, b_reg->bit_0, etc.
```

Keep in mind the following important facts when you are using fields. The detailed storage of fields is machine dependent. Arrays of fields may not be formed. Finally, trying to take the address of a field component is illegal.

In this chapter, you have seen how the related C constructs of structures, unions, and fields can be used effectively to extend the language to match any given application. When used in combination with pointers, these contructs give the programmer an essentially unlimited ability to describe and manipulate complex associations of data. You will see many examples of these ideas put to use throughout the remainder of this book.

4

Functions:
Recursion and Selection

This chapter presents some of the more advanced topics involving the use of functions. First, the technique of recursion and the differences between recursion and iteration are discussed. Then the way to approach a problem requiring a recursive solution is explained, and situations where recursion is not appropriate are cited.

The last part of the chapter contains methods for selecting alternative actions or implementations of actions by using pointers to functions. The central idea involves passing a pointer to a function, as a parameter to another function. That is, instead of supplying just a set of values for a function to use, specific algorithms to be invoked can be indicated by means of pointers to functions. The technique is easily understood and can be applied in readily recognizable types of situations.

Recursion

A function is said to be recursive if in the course of its execution, the function makes a call to itself. This call may occur inside the function, in which case the function is *directly recursive*. In other cases, a function may call another function, which in turn makes a call to the first one. This situation is known as *indirect recursion*. Of course, the chain of calls may be more involved, with several intermediate function calls before the call back to the original function. In any event, if at some point in execution, a function makes a call to itself, the function is recursive.

To users not familiar with recursion, it appears ill-defined and dangerously circular. People think the program might cycle through a never-ending sequence of function calls. This is possible, of course, but only if the function is improperly defined. The objective of a recursive function is for the program to proceed through a sequence of calls until, at a certain point, the sequence terminates.

To ensure that recursive functions are well behaved, you should observe the following guidelines:

1. Every time a recursive function is called, the program should first check to see whether some basic condition, such as a particular parameter being equal to zero, is satisfied. If this is the case, the function should stop recursing.

2. Each time the function is recursively called, one or more of the arguments passed to the function should be "simpler" in some way. That is, the parameters should be nearer the basic condition. For example, a positive integer may be smaller on each recursive call so that eventually the value reaches zero.

These guidelines are illustrated by two examples. Perhaps the factorial function is the best-known example of recursion. The factorial function is defined in terms of a recurrence relation.

```
fact(Ø) = 1

fact(n) = n * fact(n - 1), for positive integers n
```

The definition suggests immediately how the factorial function can be coded in C to meet the two required conditions.

```
int fact(n) /* compute factorial of n, nonnegative integer n */
int n;
{
    if (n == Ø)            /* basic condition */
        return(1);
    else                   /* recurse */
        return(n * fact(n - 1));
}
```

Notice how this code follows the two guidelines set forth at the beginning of this section. If a basic condition, the parameter being zero, is met, the recursion stops. If this condition is not met, the function recurses with a smaller parameter being passed to the called function each time. Eventually, the parameter reaches zero, which triggers the termination condition.

A diagram provides a clear picture of the precise series of function calls. Pick a value of n for which you want to compute the factorial and follow explicitly the series of function calls and returns. This procedure is shown in figure 4.1, for the case n = 4. In the diagram, the initial value n = 4, which is passed to the factorial function, is shown in the upper-left portion of the figure, labeled *Input*. The value of fact(4) is evaluated as 4 times the value of fact(3), thus generating the first recursive call. The series of recursive calls continues until the bottom-most box, labeled fact(0), is reached. At this point, the basic condition result of 1 is returned to its calling function fact(1). The series of called functions then returns values (in the opposite order of invocation) until the final value of 24 is determined for fact(4), as shown in the upper-right portion of the diagram, labeled *Output*.

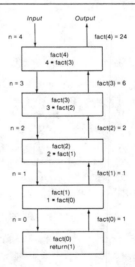

Fig. 4.1. Recursive evaluation of fact(4).

The explanation in this text is based on the assumption that only nonnegative values are passed to the function `fact`. If desired, this restriction can be enforced by having applications call a separate initialization function, rather than `fact` itself.

```
/* initialization of factorial computation */
int init_fact(n)
{
    if (n < 0)
        {
        printf("Error: negative value passed to init_fact\n");
        return(n);
        }
    else
        return(fact(n));
}
```

Using this code makes more sense than including the error check in fact itself because the test needs to be made only once. If the test is part of fact, the check is made unnecessarily during each recursive call. Of course, this same technique can be used in other similar situations.

For a second example of recursion, consider the Fibonacci numbers, which are defined as follows:

fib(0) = fib(1) = 1

fib(n) = fib(n - 1) + fib(n - 2), for integer n > 1

Each Fibonacci number is the sum of the preceding two Fibonacci numbers. To start, the first two numbers are both defined to be 1. Therefore, the next number in the sequence, fib(2), is 1 + 1 or 2. Likewise, fib(3) is 2 + 1 = 3, fib(4) is 3 + 2 = 5, and so on. The general structure of this definition is similar to the factorial case but has one important difference: the recursion involves making calls to two copies of the function at each step. This difference has dramatic effects in terms of execution time and computational complexity.

The coding of this problem is done in a straightforward fashion.

```
int fib(n)   /* nth Fibonacci number, nonnegative integer n */
int n;
{
    if (n == 0 || n == 1)          /* basic condition */
        return(1);
    else                           /* recurse */
        return(fib(n - 1) + fib(n - 2));
}
```

A diagram showing the recursive calling hierarchy for this function for the fourth Fibonacci number is shown in figure 4.2. As in the last figure, the initial call to the recursive function is labeled *Input*. To compute fib(4), the program must compute both fib(3) and fib(2). As shown, the computation of fib(3) requires the results for fib(2) and fib(1). Thus, fib(2) is calculated twice. Further inspection of the figure shows that fib(1) is calculated three times and fib(0) is calculated twice. The return values from all these function calls percolate back up to the initial box for fib(4), finally yielding the resulting value of 5, which is shown as *Output*. The figure makes clear that this method of solution is impractical for large values for n. The problem is one of a tremendous duplication of effort; the same functions are recalculated several times. Because each call to f ib makes two calls to itself, the number of calls explodes geometrically, resulting in a prohibitive execution time when n is large.

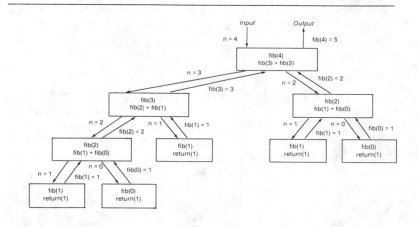

Fig. 4.2. Recursive evaluation of fib(4).

Iteration

Although the preceding two examples have served as nice conceptual examples of the recursion process, they are in fact better solved by the nonrecursive process of iteration. *Iteration* is simply the repeated execution of a block of code with local variables controlling the number of times the block is executed. C provides the constructs for, while, and do to develop structured iterative loops. Of course, goto with labels can also be used, but this practice is generally frowned upon because of its unstructured and often hard-to-understand control flow.

To turn a recursive solution into an iterative solution usually requires the introduction of one or more local variables to count or otherwise control the process. In the case of the factorial, the obvious solution is

```
int fact_it(n) /* iterative version of factorial function */
int n;
{
    int count, result;

    /* iterative loop */
    for (count = result = 1; count <= n; ++count)
        result *= count;

    /* return to caller */
    return(result);
}
```

This version is faster than the recursive solution because the iterative version avoids the overhead of passing arguments and returning values involved in the series of function calls and returns.

In the case of the Fibonacci numbers, the savings in time is much more dramatic. Not only is the exponential number of function invocations eliminated, but the tremendous duplication of effort is removed. Thus, the following iterative function is far more efficient. The basic idea is to introduce two local variables that retain the values of the two most recently calculated Fibonacci numbers. These local variables can then be repeatedly summed until you reach the final result.

```
int fib_it(n)  /* iterative version of Fibonacci numbers */
int n;
{
    /* introduce local iterative variables last, prev,
          count: last holds last Fibonacci number computed,
          prev holds Fibonacci number previous to last,
          count controls iterative loop */
    int last = 1, prev = 1, count;
    int result;

    if (n == 0 il n == 1)          /* basic condition */
        result = 1;
```

```
    else                         /* iterative loop */
        for (count = 2; count <= n; ++count)
            {
            result = prev + last;
            prev = last;
            last = result;
            }

    /* return to caller */
    return(result);
}
```

The Choice between Recursion and Iteration

As a general rule, you should avoid recursion when an iterative solution is easy to find. These situations are common when the problem can be stated in terms of a recurrence relation, as in the case of both the factorial and the Fibonacci problems. Conversely, recursion is the preferred method of solution when an iterative method is difficult to construct. Indeed, in some cases a recursive solution is almost trivial, and an iterative solution is extremely hard to find. Recursion is also the best method when the underlying data structures in the problem are themselves recursive. This type of problem is illustrated in Chapter 6, which discusses trees and forests, and in the chapters dealing with graphics applications.

Recursion in Action: The Towers of Hanoi

The famous puzzle, The Towers of Hanoi, is easy to state but extremely hard to solve unless recursion is used. As shown in figure 4.3, you have three rods (towers) on which n round disks can be stacked on top of each other, like some children's toys. Initially, all the disks are on the first rod (tower A) and are arranged so that the diameters of the disks increase from the top to the bottom of the stack. The object of the puzzle is to devise a sequence of disk moves so that the disks end up on the third rod (tower C) in the same sequence as they were on tower A. The second rod (tower

B) can be used for intermediate disk moves. Only two restrictions are placed on the movement of disks.

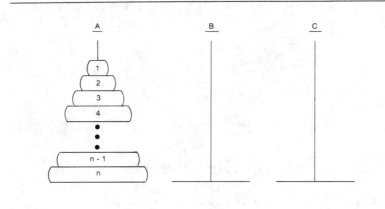

*Fig. 4.3. The Towers of Hanoi:
Initial disk positions.*

1. Only one disk can be moved at a time.

2. At no time can any disk be placed on top of a smaller disk.

To nonrecursive thinkers, this problem causes much head-scratching and pondering. On the other hand, the recursive solution is so simple that it seems almost magical. The solution proceeds as follows. If you have only one disk, it can be transferred directly from A to C. If you have more than one disk, a method must exist for legally transferring, according to the two stated rules, a stack of n - 1 disks from one tower to another. This method then can be applied to the case of n disks where n is greater than 1. (Notice how the proposed solution has been stated in such a way that recursion can be applied.)

Consider the three-step process illustrated in figure 4.4. As shown in part a, in the first step, n - 1 disks are transferred from tower A to tower B. This first step does not violate the first stated restriction; all n - 1 disks are not moved together as a unit, but rather are transferred legally from one tower to another. Note that although the ultimate goal is to transfer disks from A to C, you can use the same algorithm to transfer disks from any tower to any other simply by renaming the source and destination towers. Next, as shown in part b, you can move the one remaining disk (the largest one) from tower A directly to the still empty tower C. Finally, you use the first method again to move the stack of disks on tower B to tower C, as shown in part c. (As in the first step, this is actually a series of smaller steps involving the movement of only one disk at a time.) This step presents no problem because the only disk on C is the largest one. This solution achieves the desired result of stacking the disks in the correct order on tower C.

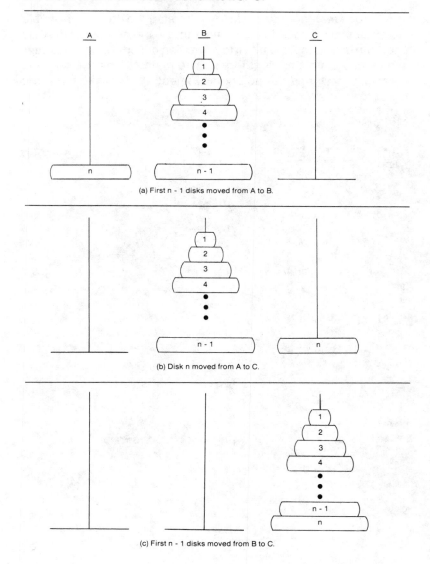

(a) First n - 1 disks moved from A to B.

(b) Disk n moved from A to C.

(c) First n - 1 disks moved from B to C.

Fig. 4.4. The Towers of Hanoi: Recursive algorithm.

Note that the preceding discussion is cast in the standard form for a recursive algorithm. The trivial case (one disk) can be solved directly. Otherwise, you make calls to a function with a "simpler" parameter value (one fewer disks). Eventually, you reach the case of only one disk, and the recursion stops.

The C code for this example follows. To start the process, a simple main function reads from the command line the number of disks to use, then makes the initial call to a function called towers. This towers function implements the recursive method, and the function move_disk performs the actual movement of the disks from one tower to another.

```c
#include <stdio.h>

/* if necessary, define void type */
#define void    int

/* define maximum number of disks allowed */
#define MAX     9

/* code for tower names */
char    code[3] = {'A', 'B', 'C'};
/* code for empty tower position */
#define EMPTY   0

/* global variables */
int     disks;          /* number of disks */
int     pos[3][MAX];    /* disk position array */
int     nest = 0;       /* nesting level */

main(argc, argv)
int     argc;
char    **argv;
/* main starts Towers of Hanoi program, command line
            argument gives number of disks to use */
{
    int     i, j;
    void    towers();
```

```
/* obtain number of disks to move */
if (argc != 2)
    {
    printf("Specify number of disks to use in command
          line\n");
    exit(1);
    }
else
    disks = atoi(argv[1]);

/* error check */
if (disks <= 0)
    {
    printf("Error: nonpositive number of disks
          specified\n");
    exit(1);
    }

/* announce the problem */
printf("The Towers of Hanoi: %d Disks\n\n", disks);

/* initialize disk positions */
for (i = 0; i < 3; ++i)
    for (j = 0; j < disks; ++j)
        if (i == 0)
            pos[i][j] = j + 1;
        else
            pos[i][j] = EMPTY;

/* print initial disk positions */
printf("          A B C\n");
printf("          - - -\n");
for (j = 0; j < disks; ++j)
printf("%11.1d %d %d\n", pos[0][j], pos[1][j],
       pos[2][j]);
printf("\n");

/* invoke recursive solution */
towers(disks, 0, 1, 2);
}
```

```
void     towers(n, src, mid, dst)
int      n, src, mid, dst;
/* towers transfers n disks from source tower to
          destination tower using intermediate
          tower as required
    n    => number of disks to move
    src  => source tower
    mid  => intermediate tower
    dst  => destination tower
*/
{
    int      i;
    void     move_disk();

    nest += 1;
    /*  indicate nesting level and call to towers */
    for (i = 0; i < nest; ++i)
         printf(" ");
    printf("call towers(%d, %c, %c, %c)\n", n,
         code[src], code[mid], code[dst]);

    /* recursive method */
    if (n == 1)        /* basic case */
         move_disk(src, dst);
    else               /* recurse with smaller argument */
         {
         towers(n - 1, src, dst, mid);
         move_disk(src, dst);
         towers(n - 1, mid, src, dst);
         }

    /* done */
    for (i = 0; i < nest; ++i)
         printf(" ");
    printf("exit towers(%d, %c, %c, %c)\n", n,
          code[src], code[mid], code[dst]);
    nest -= 1;
    return;
}
```

```
void     move_disk(src, dst)
int      src, dst;
/* move_disk moves one disk from source tower to
                destination tower and prints the move
     src => source tower
     dst => destination tower
*/
{

     int i = 0, j = 0;

     /* find starting location of disk */
     while (pos[src][i] == EMPTY)
          i++;

     /* find location to be moved to */
     while (pos[dst][j] == EMPTY && j < disks)
          j++;
     j -= 1;

     /* move disk from source to destination position */
     printf("\nMove disk #%d from %c to %c:\n\n",
          pos[src][i], code[src], code[dst]);
     pos[dst][j] = pos[src][i];
     pos[src][i] = EMPTY;

     /* print new disk positions */
     printf("          A B C\n");
     printf("          - - -\n");
     for (j = 0; j < disks; ++j)
          printf("%11.1d %d %d\n", pos[0][j], pos[1][j],
                pos[2][j]);
     printf("\n");

     /* done */
     return;
}
```

Note that the disk positions are stored in a global two-dimensional array, pos[3][MAX]. Therefore, although recursion nests the sets of parameters and local variables, you have just one central place where the disk positions are maintained. (The value of 9 for MAX has been chosen so that in the simulations shown below all the disks can be represented as single-digit numbers.)

The code includes two types of print statements. One type keeps track of the depth and nesting of the recursive calls and uses a convenient indentation scheme so that the level of nesting can be seen clearly. The other class of print statements generates a series of "snapshots" of the disks on the three towers as the simulation of the puzzle's solution progresses. Figure 4.5 shows the output of the program for the problem with three disks, and in figure 4.6 the solution is given for four disks. In these two figures, towers A, B, and C are column headers, and the positions of the disks are listed explicitly. The number 1 represents the smallest disk, with higher numbers representing progressively larger disks. A zero means the absence of any disk. You can see by the progression of the positions of the disks on the three towers that all disks eventually move from tower A to tower C, although many intermediate moves are required. Also note that the complexity of the solution (that is, the number of disk moves) increases rapidly as more disks are added to the problem.

Finally, note that the term void defines functions which do not return any value to their callers. Some compilers recognize void as a keyword. For compilers that do not, you must specify the following define statement at the top of the file:

```
#define void     int
```

Even on systems that do not recognize void, the term is good for documentation purposes. All similar functions in the remainder of this book follow this convention.

Fig. 4.5. Solution simulation: three disks.

```
The Towers of Hanoi: 3 Disks

            A B C
            - - -
            1 Ø Ø
            2 Ø Ø
            3 Ø Ø

      call towers(3, A, B, C)
        call towers(2, A, C, B)
          call towers(1, A, B, C)
```

```
Move disk #1 from A to C

        A B C
        - - -
        0 0 0
        2 0 0
        3 0 1

 exit towers(1, A, B, C)

Move disk #2 from A to B

        A B C
        - - -
        0 0 0
        0 0 0
        3 2 1

 call towers(1, C, A, B)

Move disk #1 from C to B

        A B C
        - - -
        0 0 0
        0 1 0
        3 2 0

  exit towers(1, C, A, B)
 exit towers(2, A, C, B)

Move disk #3 from A to C

        A B C
        - - -
        0 0 0
        0 1 0
        0 2 3

 call towers(2, B, A, C)
  call towers(1, B, C, A)
```

```
Move disk #1 from B to A

        A B C
        - - -
        0 0 0
        0 0 0
        1 2 3


    exit towers(1, B, C, A)

Move disk #2 from B to C

        A B C
        - - -
        0 0 0
        0 0 2
        1 0 3


    call towers(1, A, B, C)

Move disk #1 from A to C

        A B C
        - - -
        0 0 1
        0 0 2
        0 0 3


    exit towers(1, A, B, C)
    exit towers(2, B, A, C)
    exit towers(3, A, B, C)
```

Fig. 4.6. Solution simulation:
four disks.

```
The Towers of Hanoi: 4 Disks

        A B C
        - - -
        1 0 0
        2 0 0
        3 0 0
        4 0 0
```

```
call towers(4, A, B, C)
 call towers(3, A, C, B)
  call towers(2, A, B, C)
   call towers(1, A, C, B)
```

Move disk #1 from A to B

```
        A B C
        - - -
        0 0 0
        2 0 0
        3 0 0
        4 1 0
```

```
   exit towers(1, A, C, B)
```

Move disk #2 from A to C

```
        A B C
        - - -
        0 0 0
        0 0 0
        3 0 0
        4 1 2
```

```
  call towers(1, B, A, C)
```

Move disk #1 from B to C

```
        A B C
        - - -
        0 0 0
        0 0 0
        3 0 1
        4 0 2
```

```
   exit towers(1, B, A, C)
  exit towers(2, A, B, C)
```

```
Move disk #3 from A to B

              A B C
              - - -
              0 0 0
              0 0 0
              0 0 1
              4 3 2


    call towers(2, C, A, B)
     call towers(1, C, B, A)

Move disk #1 from C to A

              A B C
              - - -
              0 0 0
              0 0 0
              1 0 0
              4 3 2


    exit towers(1, C, B, A)

Move disk #2 from C to B

              A B C
              - - -
              0 0 0
              0 0 0
              1 2 0
              4 3 0


    call towers(1, A, C, B)

Move disk #1 from A to B

              A B C
              - - -
              0 0 0
              0 1 0
              0 2 0
              4 3 0
```

```
        exit towers(1, A, C, B)
       exit towers(2, C, A, B)
      exit towers(3, A, C, B)

      Move disk #4 from A to C

                A B C
                - - -
                0 0 0
                0 1 0
                0 2 0
                0 3 4


        call towers(3, B, A, C)
         call towers(2, B, C, A)
          call towers(1, B, A, C)

      Move disk #1 from B to C

                A B C
                - - -
                0 0 0
                0 0 0
                0 2 1
                0 3 4


        exit towers(1, B, A, C)

      Move disk #2 from B to A

                A B C
                - - -
                0 0 0
                0 0 0
                0 0 1
                2 3 4


        call towers(1, C, B, A)
```

```
Move disk #1 from C to A

        A B C
        - - -
        0 0 0
        0 0 0
        1 0 0
        2 3 4


 exit towers(1, C, B, A)
exit towers(2, B, C, A)

Move disk #3 from B to C

        A B C
        - - -
        0 0 0
        0 0 0
        1 0 3
        2 0 4


call towers(2, A, B, C)
 call towers(1, A, C, B)

Move disk #1 from A to B

        A B C
        - - -
        0 0 0
        0 0 0
        0 0 3
        2 1 4


 exit towers(1, A, C, B)

Move disk #2 from A to C

        A B C
        - - -
        0 0 0
        0 0 2
        0 0 3
        0 1 4
```

```
call towers(1, B, A, C)

Move disk #1 from B to C

        A B C
        - - -
        0 0 1
        0 0 2
        0 0 3
        0 0 4

    exit towers(1, B, A, C)
    exit towers(2, A, B, C)
    exit towers(3, B, A, C)
    exit towers(4, A, B, C)
```

Function Selection

Functions perform a common set of actions on different sets of parameters. No matter what specific values are passed to a function through its argument list, the specified built-in actions are performed. This feature, of course, is one of the main benefits of using functions, because part of a problem can be encapsulated into a unit and activated with varying sets of input data. Thus, as long as the algorithm is well defined, it can be invoked in many different instances according to the values of the parameters.

Another technique available in C provides an even greater capability to affect the value returned by a function. In contrast to the typical situation cited, you can alter parts of the function's actions as well as the parameter values that the function is to use. This technique, which is referred to as *function selection*, is accomplished through the use of pointers to functions.

Chapter 1 presents a top-down style of coding, which produces large functions made up of calls to other smaller functions. Each smaller function performs some specific task that contributes to the total work of the large function. Because all these small function names are listed in the text of the large function, the small functions are, in effect, "frozen" into the code as if you had hard coded a numerical value into the function instead of passing in an arbitrary value as a parameter. If you want to make the large function more generic, you can replace the specific instance of one subfunction by a pointer to a function that is passed to the large function through the function's parameter list. Then, depending on the pointer value passed, different functions are selected.

A specific example will clarify these points. Consider writing a function that lists in tabular form the values of an arbitrary int function over some range of values. The specific functions to be evaluated are selected by passing a function pointer to the generic table-generating function.

```
void    table(fp, lo, hi, inc)
int     (*fp)(), lo, hi, inc;
{

    /* check parameter values */
    if (lo >= hi)
        {
        printf("Error: low value greater than high value\n");
        return;
        }
    if (inc <= 0)
        {
        printf("Error: nonpositive increment value\n");
        return;
        }

    /* construct table */
    while (lo <= hi)
        {
        printf("%d, %d\n", lo, (*fp)(lo));
        lo += inc;
        }

    /* done */
    return;
}
```

The new elements in this function relate to the declaration and use of the function pointer, fp. Consider first the declaration

```
    int (*fp)();      /* correct */
```

This statement says that *fp corresponds to a function that returns an element of type int. The extra set of parentheses here is required. Without these parentheses you have

```
int *fp();        /* wrong!! */
```

This statement says that fp is a function which returns an element which is a pointer to an element of type int and is not at all what is intended. C has no shorthand for indicating pointers to functions (as the language does with pointers to structures), so the extra set of parentheses must be used.

Similarly, in the body of the function, you see the quantity,

```
(*fp)(lo)
```

Because *fp is the name of a function, this line is simply the invocation of that function with an argument value of lo. The function that has been passed as an argument to table is selected at this point.

To use this table generator, all you do is make a call to table with the name of the target function as the first parameter in the list.

```
/* make a table of the values of function f1 */
table(f1, 0, 10, 1);
```

You do not need to take the address of f1 in the call. The compiler knows that this call is a function selection and passes the address of f1 to table. (Note that this convention is similar to the one in which the name of an array corresponds to the address of the zero element of that array.) The function f1 itself is described just like any other function of an int argument that returns an int value. For example, you can have

```
/* candidate one, general quadratic function */
int f1(x)
int x;
{
    return(P*x*x + Q*x + R);
}
```

The constants P, Q, and R have been #defined elsewhere.

You can now just as easily define other functions for which you want tables generated, for example,

```
/* candidate two, mod P function */
int f2(x)
int x;
{
    return(x % P);
}
```

A table of values for this function can then be generated by

```
table(f2, 0, 10, 1);
```

Thus, although f1 and f2 are different functions, the single table routine is adequate for handling both.

This section concludes discussion of the set of advanced features that the C language has to offer an applications programmer. In the remaining chapters, these features will be used extensively to build and manipulate complex data structures as well as to develop two libraries of graphics and advanced user interface functions.

5
Linked Lists

Linked lists, whatever their form, are among the most important types of data structures. These lists are extremely useful in the design of advanced applications programs. Much of the foundation for understanding linked lists has already been laid in Chapters 2 and 3.

In this chapter, the basic concepts behind the linked list structure and implementation in C are given first. Next, several operators useful for manipulating linked lists are defined. Then some useful variations of the linked list structure are described. Finally, ways linked lists can be generalized to form other more complex combinations of data are presented.

Linked List Building Blocks

A *linked list*, or *list* for short, is an ordered sequence of elements called *nodes*. A list has a beginning, or *head*, and an end, or *tail*. Every node on the list is the same type, although that type can take different forms.

A central property of linked lists is their dynamic nature. Nodes can be added to or removed from a list at any time. Because the number of nodes cannot be predicted before run time, you should use pointers, rather than arrays, to achieve an efficient and reliable implementation.

Nodes

Each node of a list consists of two parts. The first part holds the data. This data can be a simple variable or, more generally, a structure (or pointer to a structure) of some type. The second part of the node is a pointer that indicates the location of the next node of the list. Therefore, the nodes of a list can be conveniently implemented by a self-referential, or recursive, structure.

As a simple example, consider the case where a single integer variable is to be stored at each node of the list. This can be implemented by defining a node as follows:

```
/* simple list node containing a single integer */
struct simple
    {
    int         item;
    struct simple *next;
    };

typedef struct simple simple_t;
```

In this case, the integer variable item holds the actual data in each node, and the pointer variable next holds the address of the next node. The list that this structure gives rise to is diagrammed in figure 5.1. As shown in the figure, the item variable is in the first component of each node, while the next pointer, symbolized by the arrow pointing to the following node, is contained in the second component of each node.

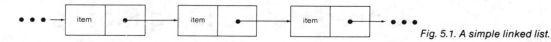

Fig. 5.1. A simple linked list.

A more general situation is the case where each node of a list can contain several pieces of data. Here, defining a structure type that corresponds to the data to be stored at each node is more sensible. This method is indicated in the following node type definition:

```
/* general list node, first version */
struct genl
    {
    info_t      item;
    struct genl *next;
    };

typedef struct genl genl_t;
```

The structure type info_t must have been previously defined to correspond to the data to be stored at each node. A list formed with this type of node also looks like the diagram in figure 5.1. However, each item is a complete structure rather than a single integer variable.

Although the preceding structure seems to be generally useful, this kind of implementation has two problems, both of which have to do with the operations to be performed on the lists. For each type of list built, you must specify all the individual component assignments involved in transferring information to and from nodes. Therefore, your list manipulation functions must be rewritten for every type of list you construct. This practice is wasteful because the same generic operations are performed on all types of lists regardless of the form of the data stored at each node.

You can partially solve this problem by layering the data assignment process with a specially defined assign function. The concept is based on the fact that you really want to be able to write statements like

```
    s1 = s2;            /* wrong */
```

where s1 and s2 are both structures. In C, of course, you cannot perform operations in that manner on structures as a whole. You can assign only a single structure component in each C statement. You can, however, mimic this operation by writing

```
    assign(s1, s2);      /* right */
    info_t *s1, *s2;
    {
        /* assign each component of struct 2 to struct 1 */
            . . .

    }
```

The assign function is defined to carry out the detailed transfer of the individual structure components from s2 to s1. Defining a new assign function according to each list type is simple. You can build a series of generic list manipulation functions that use assign. Then you simply #include the proper assign function for the type of list element you want to use.

However, this approach may have a second problem: performance. If the structure is at all complicated, you will be transferring much data among different memory locations. However, you need to transfer only the addresses of the blocks of data corresponding to the structures.

Solving these related problems leads to the preferred way of building a list node. To build a list node, use a structure composed of a pair of pointers. The first pointer points to the data associated with the node (normally a structure of some type); and the second pointer, as before, gives the address where the next list node can be found. The code is as follows:

```
/* general list node, all-pointer version */
struct node
    {
    info_t      *item;
    struct node *next;
    };

    typedef struct node node_t;
```

This method leads to a linked list structure as diagrammed in figure 5.2.

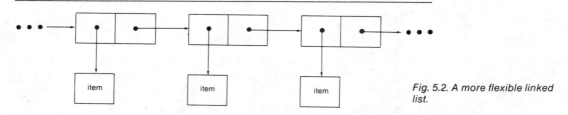

Fig. 5.2. A more flexible linked list.

Manipulation of Linked Lists

The manipulation of linked lists involves allocating storage for nodes (using the MALLOC or CALLOC macro) and assigning data and/or pointers so that the list is properly formed. First, however, the question of a list's *boundary conditions* must be decided. That is, how are the head and the tail of a list to be indicated? The representation of the tail is no problem, because you can use a NULL pointer to indicate that no more elements are in the list (see the diagram in fig. 5.3).

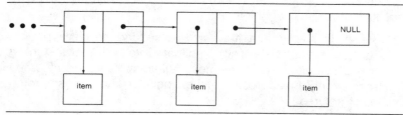

Fig. 5.3. Using a NULL pointer to indicate the end of a list.

However, several different approaches can be used to mark the head of the list. The most direct approach is to define a simple pointer variable to hold the starting address of the list. Although this technique works, defining a special header node is usually more convenient. This header node acts as an interface between the list and the functions that manipulate it. For example, a simple approach here is to use the same structure for the head as for all the other nodes (see fig. 5.4). In this method, the next element of the head node holds the starting address of the list. The item portion of the header remains unassigned. Although this allocation results in a small amount of wasted space (the unused item portion), this method is sometimes convenient because it allows many list manipulation functions to be constructed with a certain degree of symmetry.

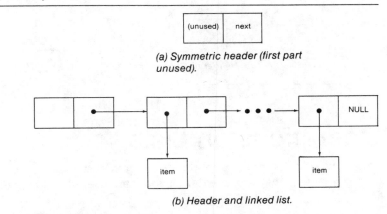

(a) Symmetric header (first part unused).

(b) Header and linked list.

Fig. 5.4. Using a symmetric header.

Another possibility is to define for the header a separate structure that is custom-made to hold exactly the information required. This separate structure not only eliminates the small waste, but also allows you to add extra information about the list, such as the current number of elements in the list and a pointer to the last element of the list. The C code for such a header node definition looks like this:

```
/* custom header node, general list using all pointers */
struct head
      {
      int      length;        /* current length of list */
      node_t   *first, *last; /* pointers to first and last elements */
      };

typedef struct head head_t;
```

A list constructed with this custom header node is diagrammed in figure 5.5. This technique is the one that is most often used in this book.

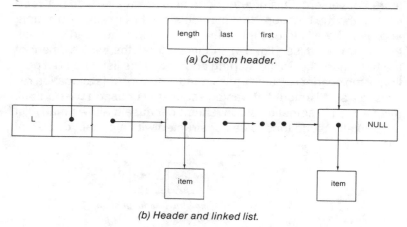

(a) Custom header.

(b) Header and linked list.

Fig. 5.5. Using a custom header.

Operations on Lists

This section includes the important concepts and actual C code for several useful types of operations that can be applied to linked lists.

Creating a New List

The first operation to be considered creates a new list. The only actions that must be performed are to allocate memory for the header node and to set all the node's components to their appropriate values. Use both the custom header and the all-pointer style of list nodes. The function that creates a new list can be written as

```
/* create a new list */
head_t  *create()
{
    head_t  *new;

    /* attempt memory allocation */
    if (new = MALLOC(head_t))
        {
```

```
/* allocation OK, initialize component values */
new->length = 0;
new->first = new->last = NULL;
}

/* return address of new list */
return(new);
}
```

Note that this routine returns the address where the newly created header node can be found. To indicate an error, the routine returns a NULL pointer if the allocation is not successful.

Inserting a New Element at the Beginning of a List

The next operation inserts a new element at the beginning of a list. Consider a list that already has some elements, as diagrammed in figure 5.6a. The required steps are as follows:

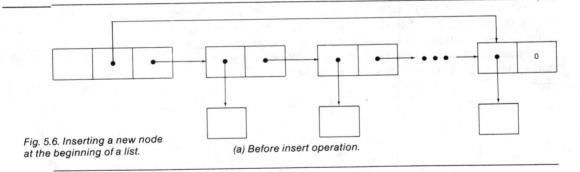

Fig. 5.6. Inserting a new node at the beginning of a list.

(a) Before insert operation.

1. Create storage for a new list node.

2. Assign appropriate pointer values to the new node.

3. Assign new values to the components of the header node.

Because the allocation and subsequent initialization of general list nodes occurs frequently, first define a list node instantiation function (as explained in Chapter 3). This function allocates storage for a node and assigns values to the node's components according to the values of the parameters that are passed to the function, as follows:

```
/* instantiate new node */
node_t *inst_node(val, ptr)
info_t *val;
node_t *ptr;
{
    node_t *new;

    /* attempt allocation and assignments */
    if (new = MALLOC(node_t))
        {
        new->item = val;
        new->next = ptr;
        }

    /* done */
    return(new);
}
```

As in the previous list creation function, this function returns the address of the new node and flags an allocation error by returning a value of NULL.

Given this function, constructing an insert function is simple. As shown schematically in figure 5.6b, you need to assign the value of the header's current first pointer to the next component of the new node. Then update the first and length components of the header itself. The C code is written as follows:

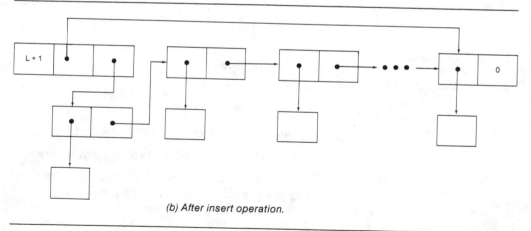

(b) After insert operation.

```
/* definitions for return value of function */
#define TRUE    1
#define FALSE   0
#define BOOLEAN int /* TRUE or FALSE */

/* insert data at beginning of list */
BOOLEAN insert(data, list)
info_t  *data;
head_t  *list;
{
    node_t  *new, *inst_node();

    /* attempt insert operation */
    if (new = inst_node(data, list->first))
        {
        /* allocation OK, assign new header pointer */
        list->first = new;         /* link in new node */
        if (list->length == 0) /* if this is the first node, */
            list->last = new;    /* then set last pointer to new */
        list->length++;            /* update list length */
        return(TRUE);
        }
    else
        /* flag allocation error */
        return(FALSE);
}
```

Note that the function also checks to see whether this is the first node to be inserted in the list. If so, the last pointer (which had a value of NULL) also should be set to the address of the newly allocated node.

The insert function is defined so that it returns a BOOLEAN value of TRUE or FALSE, depending on the success or failure of the allocation. If the allocation of new node space is not successful, the function leaves the original list intact and flags this error condition by returning a FALSE. The calling function can then check the returned value and proceed accordingly. Many list manipulation functions use this simple convention.

One detail concerning the use of pointers in the preceding function must be stressed. The only memory allocated by insert is for the list cell itself. The caller of insert has the responsibility of allocating memory and initializing the data to which item points.

Thus, when this function is called again, some other memory already must have been allocated and written to (by the calling function) in order to hold data for another item in the list. Note that these comments also apply to the other similar list manipulation functions presented in this chapter.

Appending a New Item to the End of a List

A second common operation appends a new item to the end of a list. The "before" and "after" situations for this operation are diagrammed in figure 5.7. You know where to find the current last node in the list by means of the last pointer, which is maintained in the header block. Thus, you only have to allocate memory for a new node and rearrange pointers accordingly. As in the previous case, you can construct the function so that it flags an allocation error by returning a FALSE value. The code is as follows:

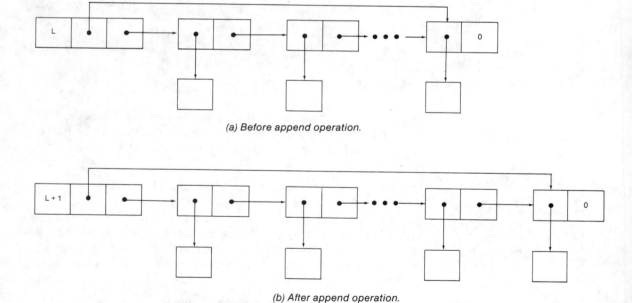

(a) Before append operation.

(b) After append operation.

Fig. 5.7. Appending a new node to the end of a list.

```
/* append data to end of list */
BOOLEAN append(data, list)
info_t *data;
head_t *list;
{
    node_t *new, *inst_node();

    /* append data to end of list */
    if (new = inst_node(data, NULL))
        {
        /* allocation OK, append data item */
        if (list->length)              /* if the list is not empty, */
            list->last->next = new;    /*  link in new node. */
        else                           /* otherwise */
            list->first = new;         /*  set first pointer to new */
        list->last = new;              /* update last pointer */
        list->length++;                /* update list length */
        return(TRUE);
        }
    else
        /* flag allocation problem */
        return(FALSE);
}
```

Deleting Nodes

At times, you probably will want to delete nodes from a list. Consider writing a function that deletes the first node from a list. First,
rearrange pointers as diagrammed in figure 5.8. After the appropriate information has been entered properly, you can return the
space occupied by the deleted node to the operating system. This
space is then made available for use. This process is accomplished by a call to the free function. In view of what was stated
about the insert function, you also will want to return a pointer to
the item being unlinked from the list so that the calling program
can free that memory, too. (If, however, some other part of the program also points to this data, you will not want to delete the information.) The code for this operation looks like this:

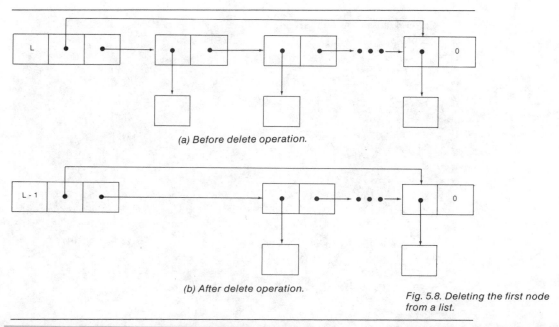

(a) Before delete operation.

(b) After delete operation.

Fig. 5.8. Deleting the first node from a list.

```
/* delete first node from list */
/* check list->length before calling this function */
info_t  *delete(list)
head_t  *list;
{
    node_t  *temp;
    info_t  *data;

    /* delete first node */
    temp = list->first;            /* save pointer value */
    data = temp->item;             /* save pointer to item */
    list->first = temp->next;      /* reassign first pointer */
    list->length--;                /* adjust current length */
    if (list->length == 0)         /* if none left, */
        list->last = NULL;         /*   set last pointer to NULL */
    free((char *)temp);            /* free node storage */

    /* return address of unlinked item */
    return(data);
}
```

Of course, deleting the first node in a list makes sense only if the list has at least one node. The variable list->length always holds the current number of nodes in the list. Thus, to avoid a possible runtime error, the application should first check that the value of list->length is greater than zero before calling this delete function.

The preceding operations constitute a core of useful functions that can be applied to simple lists of this type. Of course, you can create and write other generally useful or more specialized functions that perform different operations on lists. These operations might include sorting the list by a specified method, finding the presence or location of a particular element, and adding or removing a node at an arbitrary position in the list. By using the previous functions as a guide, you should find constructing any type of list manipulation function relatively straightforward.

Doubly Linked Lists

When you manipulate lists, being able to traverse them in both directions is often convenient. Sometimes you need to move through a list from the end to the beginning by following a series of pointers. This capability is implemented easily by increasing the information stored in each list node. In addition to the next pointer, which contains the address of the next node in the list, you also include a prev pointer, which holds the address of the previous node. In that way, you get the following structure for list nodes:

```
/* doubly linked list node */
struct dbly
    {
    info_t      *item;
    struct dbly *next, *prev;
    };

typedef struct dbly dbly_t;
```

The header node form that you have been using does not need to be changed to accommodate doubly linked lists. However, you do need to change the data types of the first and last pointers from node_t to dbly_t. This alteration leads to a new header type definition, as follows:

```
/* header for doubly linked lists */
struct head2
    {
    int     length;
    dbly_t *first, *last;
    };

typedef struct head2 head2_t;
```

You also need a new convention for the value of prev in the first node in the list. You cannot use the address of the header for the value of prev because headers are type head2_t, and the prev pointer is type dbly_t. The values of headers and prev cannot be interchanged. The obvious solution is to assign a value of NULL to prev in the first node. This assignment creates the mirror image of the previously explained practice of assigning NULL to the next pointer in the last node in a list. A schematic representation of the doubly linked list structure is shown in figure 5.9.

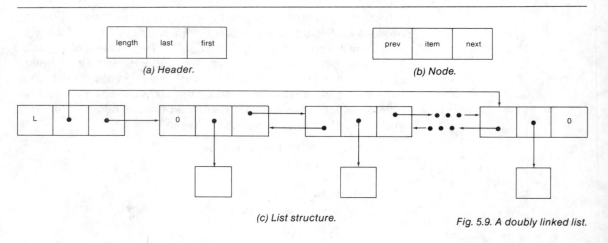

(a) Header.   (b) Node.

(c) List structure.   Fig. 5.9. A doubly linked list.

For doubly linked lists, you need to develop a new set of routines that are analogous to those for ordinary (singly linked) lists. The function to create a new doubly linked list is nearly the same as that for singly linked lists, in that you have to change only the data types of the header pointers.

```
/* create a new doubly linked list */
head2_t *crt_dbl()
{
    head2_t  *new;

    /* attempt memory allocation */
    if (new = MALLOC(head2_t))
        {
        /* allocation OK, initialize component values */
        new->length = 0;
        new->first = new->last = NULL;
        }

    /* return address of new list */
    return(new);
}
```

You also need a new instantiation function that allocates and initializes doubly linked list nodes. This function can be written as

```
/* instantiate doubly linked list node */
dbly_t *inst_dbly(data, prev, next)
info_t *data;
dbly_t *prev, *next;
{
    dbly_t  *new;

    /* attempt allocation */
    if (new = MALLOC(dbly_t))
        {
        /* allocation successful, assign pointers */
        new->item = data;
        new->prev = prev;
        new->next = next;
        }

    /* done */
    return(new);
}
```

Using this function, you can write, insert (fig. 5.10), and append (fig. 5.11) functions that operate on doubly linked lists. The general format is the same as before, but you must take care of one additional pointer (prev). The functions are written in the following way:

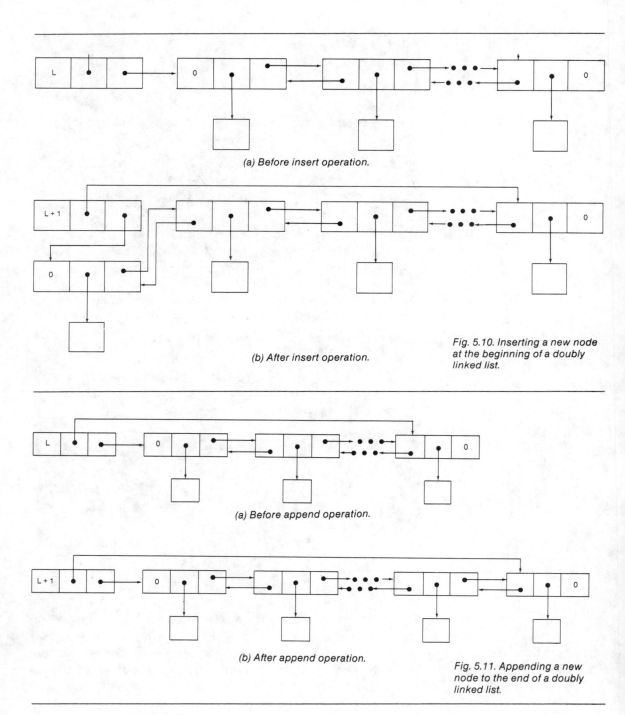

(a) Before insert operation.

(b) After insert operation.

Fig. 5.10. Inserting a new node at the beginning of a doubly linked list.

(a) Before append operation.

(b) After append operation.

Fig. 5.11. Appending a new node to the end of a doubly linked list.

```
/* insert data at beginning of doubly linked list */
BOOLEAN ins_dbl(data, list)
info_t  *data;
head2_t *list;
{
    dbly_t  *new, *inst_dbly();

    /* attempt insert operation */
    if (new = inst_dbly(data, NULL, list->first))
        {
        /* allocation OK, update values accordingly */
        if (list->length)               /* if the list is not empty, */
            list->first->prev = new;    /*  set prev of former first */
        else                            /* otherwise, */
            list->last = new;           /*  set last pointer to new */
        list->first = new;              /* link in the new node */
        list->length++;                 /* update list length */
        return(TRUE);
        }
    else
        /* flag allocation error */
        return(FALSE);
}

/* append data to end of doubly linked list */
BOOLEAN app_dbl(data, list)
info_t  *data;
head2_t *list;
{
    dbly_t  *new, *inst_dbly();

    /* append data to end of list */
    if (new = inst_dbly(data, list->last, NULL))
        {
        /* allocation OK, append data item */
        if (list->length)               /* if the list is not empty, */
            list->last->next = new;     /*   then link in new node */
        else                            /* otherwise, */
            list->first = new;          /*  set first pointer to new */
        list->last = new;               /* update last pointer */
        list->length++;                 /* update list length */
        return(TRUE);
        }
```

```
    else
        /* flag allocation problem */
        return(FALSE);
}
```

You can construct a delete function (fig. 5.12) in a manner similar to that of the construction just explained. The C code is as follows:

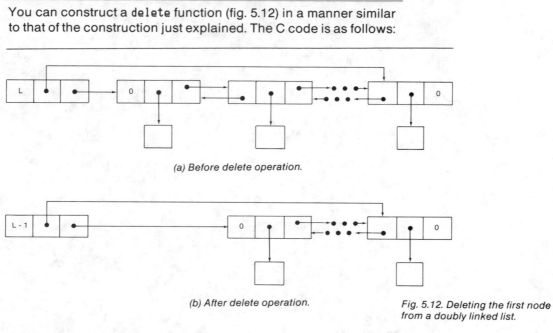

(a) Before delete operation.

(b) After delete operation.

Fig. 5.12. Deleting the first node from a doubly linked list.

```
/* delete first node from a doubly linked list */
/* check list->length before calling this function */
info_t *del_dbl(list)
head2_t *list;
{
    dbly_t  *temp;
    info_t  *data;

    /* delete first node */
    temp = list->first;              /* save pointer value */
    data = temp->item;               /* save pointer to item */
    list->first = temp->next;        /* reassign first pointer */
    list->length--;                  /* update list length */
    if (list->length)                /* if new list is not empty */
        list->first->prev = NULL;    /* flag beginning of list */
```

```
else                            /* otherwise */
    list->last = NULL;          /* set last pointer to NULL */
free((char *)temp);             /* free node storage */

/* return address of unlinked item */
return(data);
}
```

Although the code for each operation is slightly more complex than the code for ordinary lists, the extra complexity pays off when you have to perform backward list traversals.

Stacks

A *stack* is a special type of linked list. Although many types of operations can be performed on general lists, a stack has an unusual property that allows the addition and deletion of elements to be done from only one place: the *top* of the stack. If an item is added to the stack, the item is said to be *pushed* on to the stack. Similarly, when an item is removed, it is said to be *popped* from the stack. A common analogy is a stack of plates. Access to the plates is restricted to removing the top one or adding a new one to the top. Because of this property, a stack is commonly referred to as a LIFO, Last In First Out, data structure. In other words, the last item added to the stack must be the first one removed.

Stacks are widely used data structures. Whenever a series of operations is nested (that is, whenever one operation invokes another, which invokes yet another, etc.), usually the sequence of operations must be retraced in exact reverse order. In the course of the nesting, certain variables may be assigned values, and you must be able to restore the *state,* or set of values, that existed at any given time. By pushing items on to a stack and then subsequently popping the same items from the stack, you can achieve this arrangement.

Consider now the implementation of stacks in C. Because you can interact with the stack only at the top, you need to maintain a pointer to only that one node. You may still be interested, however, in the current number of elements on the stack. The following header structure is appropriate for stacks:

```
/* header for stacks */
struct lifo
    {
    int      length;
    node_t  *top;
    };

typedef struct lifo lifo_t;
```

You do not need to create a new structure type for the nodes of the stack because the general list node of the singly linked list works well.

You need to write a series of stack manipulation functions. These functions include routines for creating new stacks and pushing and popping nodes. You write these functions in a manner similar to the way explained in the section on list operators. In fact, push is nothing more than the insert function, and pop is delete. The only differences are trivial: the pointer first becomes top, and you do not have to keep track of a last pointer. The code for these stack manipulation functions follows:

```
/* create a new stack */
lifo_t  *crt_stk()
{
    lifo_t  *new;

    /* attempt memory allocation */
    if (new = MALLOC(lifo_t))
        {
        /* allocation OK, initialize component values */
        new->length = 0;
        new->top = NULL;
        }

    /* return address of new stack or flag allocation error */
    return(new);
}
```

```
/* push data on to stack */
BOOLEAN push(data, stack)
info_t *data;
lifo_t *stack;
{
    node_t *new, *inst_node();

    /* attempt push operation */
    if (new = inst_node(data, stack->top))
        {
        /* allocation OK, assign component values */
        stack->top = new;          /* set new top of stack */
        stack->length++;           /* update stack length */
        return(TRUE);
        }
    else
        /* flag allocation error */
        return(FALSE);
}

/* pop data off top of stack */
/* check stack->length before calling this function */
info_t *pop(stack)
lifo_t *stack;
{
    node_t *temp;
    info_t *data;

    /* pop the stack */
    temp = stack->top;              /* save pointer value */
    data = temp->item;              /* save the popped item */
    stack->top = temp->next;        /* reassign top pointer */
    stack->length--;                /* adjust current length */
    free((char *)temp);             /* free node storage */

    /* return address of popped item */
    return(data);
}
```

Note that, as for delete functions, pop works on the assumption that the stack is not empty.

Queues

A *queue* is another special type of list structure. An unusual property of a queue is that elements are added at one end, called the *rear*, and removed at the other end, called the *front*. These structures are used in programming situations requiring that a sequence of elements be processed in a fixed order. The processing of these elements is done in First In First Out, FIFO, order. An analogy here is a line of people waiting to pay at a cash register.

Queues arise when some fixed resource (for example, the cash register) needs to service many requesting entities (the people in line). In software systems, you may be generating information faster than it can be processed, and a backlog develops as each item waits its turn to be served. For example, you may be using a combination of keyboard entries and interactive mouse movements faster than the program can handle. Because you do not want to lose any input information, data must be stored in sequence until the system is ready to accept each item.

As you did for stacks, use an implementation based on linked lists. As with both ordinary lists and stacks, a queue is made up of a header and a linked list. In the header, you need pointers to both the front and the rear of the queue. In addition, maintaining an integer variable that keeps track of the current number of elements stored in the queue is convenient. The following structure definition is for the queue header:

```
/* header for queues */
struct fifo
    {
    int     length;
    node_t  *front, *rear;
    };

typedef struct fifo fifo_t;
```

This code is the same form as the head_t that was used for singly linked lists; only the structure component's names have been changed.

The function for creating a new queue is similar to creating other types of linked list structures.

```
/* create a new queue */
fifo_t *crt_que()
{
    fifo_t  *new;

    /* attempt allocation */
    if (new = MALLOC(fifo_t))
        {
        /* allocation successful, initialize header components */
        new->length = 0;
        new->front = new->rear = NULL;
        }

    /* done */
    return(new);
}
```

As with the other similar routines, if the routine is successful, the crt_que function returns the address of the new queue header. Otherwise, a NULL pointer flag is returned.

Once a queue has been created, you can add, or *enqueue*, elements to the rear. The following routine, which is analogous to the append function, performs the enqueue operation:

```
/* add data to rear of queue */
BOOLEAN enqueue(data, queue)
info_t *data;
fifo_t *queue;
{
    node_t  *new, *inst_node();

    /* enqueue data at rear of queue */
    if (new = inst_node(data, NULL))
        {
        /* allocation OK, proceed with enqueue operation */
        if (queue->length)              /* if queue is not empty, */
            queue->rear->next = new;  /*  link in new node */
        else                            /* otherwise */
            queue->front = new;       /* set front pointer */
        queue->rear = new;              /* update rear pointer */
        queue->length++;                /* update queue length */
        return(TRUE);
        }
```

```
    else
        /* flag allocation problem */
        return(FALSE);
}
```

You need a function that is the counterpart of enqueue, namely a function that removes data from the front of the queue. This operation, known as *dequeue*, is like the delete function.

```
/* remove data from front of queue */
/* check queue->length before calling this function */
info_t *dequeue(queue)
fifo_t *queue;
{
    node_t *temp;
    info_t *data;

    /* remove front element */
    temp = queue->front;          /* save pointer value */
    data = temp->item;            /* save pointer to item */
    queue->front = temp->next;    /* reassign front pointer */
    queue->length--;              /* adjust current length */
    if (queue->length == 0)       /* if none left, */
        queue->rear = NULL;       /*   set rear pointer to NULL */
    free((char *)temp);           /* free node storage */

    /* return address of item dequeued */
    return(data);
}
```

Lists of Lists

You have seen how to construct many types of data structures based on the linked list concept. In essence, a series of elements of some given type is placed in memory in such a way that the program can proceed from one to the next by following pointers. In the cases discussed thus far, each element is a structure (or more precisely, a pointer to a structure). However, list elements can be more complex. In particular, consider a list of which the components are themselves lists, that is, a list of lists. Such a generalization of the linked list data structure occurs frequently in software systems. For example, a list of lists forms a central part of the applications graphics system presented in Chapter 7. This section of the text describes how these data structures can be defined and manipulated.

A schematic view of the organization of a list of lists is given in figure 5.13. The basic concept is that the nodes of the main, or outer, list serve as headers for the sublists. Therefore, two kinds of dynamically adjusted quantities exist: the number of sublists and the number of elements in each sublist. Also note that all the lists involved can be singly or doubly linked. For simplicity, consider the case of a singly linked list of singly linked lists.

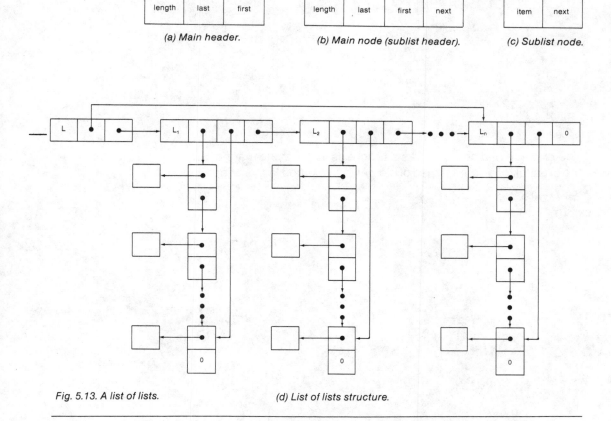

(a) Main header.   (b) Main node (sublist header).   (c) Sublist node.

Fig. 5.13. A list of lists.   (d) List of lists structure.

To implement a list of lists in C, you must first define two new data structures. First, nodes of the main list are called links (to differentiate them from the nodes of the sublists), and there is a corresponding data type, link_t. Second, the header of the main list contains pointers to the first and last link and is specified by the main_t data type:

```
/* link in main list (sublist header) */
struct link
    {
    int         length;        /* length of sublist */
    node_t      *first, *last;  /* beginning & end of sublist */
    struct link *next;          /* next link in main list */
    };

typedef struct link link_t;

/* header for main list */
struct main
    {
    int     length;        /* number of sublists */
    link_t  *first, *last;  /* beginning & end of main list */
    };

typedef struct main main_t;
```

The creation of a new list of lists proceeds in the same manner as the creation of all other types of elements explained in this chapter.

```
/* create list of lists */
main_t  *crt_lol()
{
    main_t  *new;

    /* attempt allocation */
    if (new = MALLOC(main_t))
        {
        /* allocation successful, initialize header components */
        new->length = 0;
        new->first = new->last = NULL;
        }

    /* done */
    return(new);
}
```

Next, write a function that will add a new linked list to the beginning of a list of lists. First, you need to be able to instantiate a new link.

```
/* instantiate new link */
link_t  *inst_link(first, last, next)
node_t  *first, *last;
link_t  *next;
{
    link_t  *new;

    /* attempt allocation and assignments */
    if (new = MALLOC(link_t))
        {
        new->first = first;
        new->last = last;
        new->next = next;
        }

    /* done */
    return(new);
}
```

Then you proceed as with the insert function. The new function, ins_sub, "links in" an already existing linked list whose address is given by a head_t pointer.

```
/* insert a sublist at the beginning of a list of lists */
BOOLEAN ins_sub(sub, lol)
head_t  *sub;     /* sublist header */
main_t  *lol;     /* list of lists header */
{
    link_t  *new, *inst_link();

    /* attempt insert operation */
    if (new = inst_link(sub->first, sub->last, lol->first))
        {
        /* allocation OK, assign new header pointer */
        lol->first = new;          /* link in new sublist */
        if (lol->length == 0)   /* if this is the first sublist, */
            lol->last = new;       /*   set last pointer to new */
        lol->length++;             /* update list of lists length */
        return(TRUE);
        }
    else
        /* flag allocation error */
        return(FALSE);
}
```

Finally, consider the code to insert a new node at the beginning of the first sublist in a list of lists.

```
/* insert a node at the beginning of the first sublist */
BOOLEAN ins_node(obj, lol)
node_t  *obj;
main_t  *lol;
{
    node_t  *new, *inst_node();

    /* attempt insert operation */
    if (new = inst_node(obj, lol->first->first))
        {
        /* allocation OK, assign new header pointer */
        lol->first->first = new;        /* link in new node */
        if (lol->first->length == 0) /* if first element, */
            lol->first->last = new;     /*  set last to new */
        lol->first->length++;           /* update sublist length */
        return(TRUE);
        }
    else
        /* flag allocation error */
        return(FALSE);
}
```

With a data structure as rich as the list of lists, naturally, many other conceivable operations can be defined. The preceding functions will serve as examples of how these other operations can be implemented in C.

Throughout this chapter, you have seen many variations of data structures that are derived from the linked list paradigm. As this last section has indicated, these structures can be generalized in ways that result in a hierarchy of elements. A main list can be composed of other lists, which in turn can be composed of still other lists. When the data structures become this complex, however, a new paradigm that allows hierarchies to be expressed more naturally is better. This structure, known as the tree, is the subject of the next chapter.

6
Trees

Trees are hierarchical data structures. Everyday examples of trees include company organization charts and genealogies (family trees). Because hierarchical structures are also common in software systems, trees have many applications as data structures. Because trees work well with recursive functions, the two often are found together.

This chapter presents the types of tree structures as well as several kinds of operations that can be performed on trees. Special-purpose and general-purpose tree structures and collections of trees, known as *forests*, are explained.

Introduction to Trees

A *tree*, like a linked list, is a collection of data stored in *nodes*. Nodes may be added to or deleted from a given tree as a program is executing. Unlike a linked list, however, the nodes of a tree maintain certain hierarchical relationships with each other. A typical tree structure is shown in figure 6.1.

The terminology used in discussing the structure of trees is drawn from a mixture of terms, from analogies to both biological trees and genealogies. For example, the top node of a tree is called the *root*. (As seen in fig. 6.1, tree structures are normally drawn as upside-down biological trees with the root, labeled R, at the top.) The nodes that do not have any other nodes branching out are called *leaf nodes*. Relationships among the nodes of a tree also can be described by using terms that define family relationships, such as *parent*, *child*, *sibling*, *ancestor*, and *descendent* nodes. For example, the root is the ancestor of all other nodes, but leaf nodes have no descendants. In figure 6.1, node A is the parent of the leaf nodes B and C, B and C are children of node A, and nodes B and C are siblings.

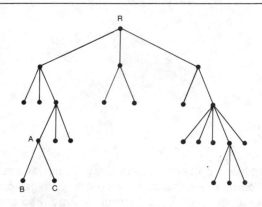

Fig. 6.1. A tree structure.

Node Ordering

In linked lists, the ordering of the nodes is simple and straightforward. A list's header points to the first node, and all other nodes follow in linear succession. For trees, the situation is more complex. Because a node can have many sibling and child nodes, the order of the nodes may not be straightforward.

Node ordering is important. For instance, sometimes you must search through all the nodes of a tree. Only if you follow a well-defined path are you assured of "visiting" each node just once. Any method of ordering the nodes of a tree is purely arbitrary, but some ordering schemes have useful interpretations beyond a simple listing of the nodes. The important point is that the order must be precise and well-defined.

Methods for Ordering the Nodes

Three popular methods for ordering the nodes of a tree are *preorder*, *in-order*, and *postorder*. The methods are similar, and each is defined recursively. Each method considers any given tree to be composed of the root and its subtrees (see fig. 6.2). Each subtree has its own root and set of subtrees.

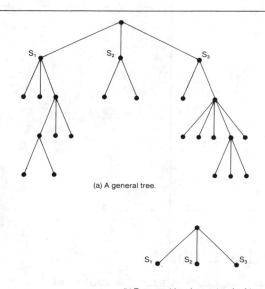

(a) A general tree.

Fig. 6.2. Divisions of a tree.

(b) Tree considered as root and subtrees.

Preorder Listing

Consider first the algorithm for preorder listing, which can be described recursively as follows:

1. If a tree is composed of a single node, the preorder listing consists of just that single node.

2. If a tree consists of more than one node, the preorder listing consists of the root, followed by the preorder listing of each subtree in left-to-right order.

This description follows the standard form for recursive algorithms. A basic condition is checked first: whether the tree is composed of only a single node. If this condition is not satisfied, the algorithm is called again with a "simpler" case to solve (a subtree of the original tree). The basic condition is met when the leaf nodes of the original tree are reached.

Note that in this case the recursive nature of the data structure leads directly into a recursive solution, as is often the case with problems involving tree structures. The nodes of the tree in figure 6.3 are numbered according to the preorder method.

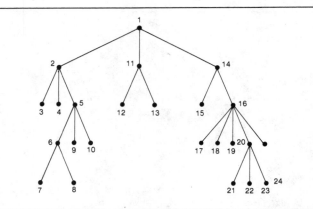

Fig. 6.3. Preorder listing.

In-Order Listing

In the recursive descent from the root to all the leaf nodes, the preorder system always lists the root node first. This choice, of course, is arbitrary. The other two ordering methods make different choices. The in-order listing of nodes is defined as follows:

1. If a tree is composed of only a single node, the in-order listing consists of just that single node.

2. If a tree consists of more than one node, the in-order listing consists of the in-order listing of the leftmost child subtree, followed by that root, and then the in-order listing of each remaining subtree, in left-to-right order.

The in-order listing of the previous example is shown in figure 6.4. Note that in this case, the first node is determined by descending the leftmost child subtrees until a leaf node is reached. As shown, this leaf node's parent then is labeled as the second node. Then, still following the definition in the previous paragraph, the labeling continues with the in-order listing of each remaining subtree.

Postorder Listing

The postorder listing differs from the previous two by listing the root node after all the subtrees have been considered.

1. If a tree is composed of only a single node, the postorder listing consists of just that single node.

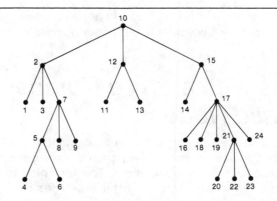

Fig. 6.4. In-order listing.

2. If a tree consists of more than one node, the postorder listing consists of the postorder listing of each subtree, in left-to-right order, followed by the root.

The postorder listing of the example tree is shown in figure 6.5. Here, as shown, the leaf nodes are listed early. Parent nodes are not listed until all of their child nodes have been listed. Notice that the root of the entire tree is listed last.

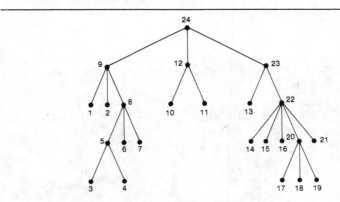

Fig. 6.5. Postorder listing.

Implementations of Trees

As with linked lists, you use a recursive structure definition to implement trees in C. You have one of two possible conditions to consider when you implement trees. You may have a fixed or maximum number of child nodes that any node can have, or you may have a variable or unpredictable number of child nodes for each node.

Trees with a Fixed Number of Child Nodes

First, consider the simpler case of a fixed number of child nodes. This restriction does not affect the size of the tree because you still may have any number of generations. The fixed number limits only the multiplicity, the rate of growth, of the tree. The simplest example is a *binary tree* in which each node can have zero, one, or two child nodes (see fig. 6.6). Each child node is referred to as the left or the right child. An appropriate data structure for a binary tree node is

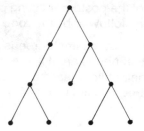

Fig. 6.6. A binary tree.

```
/* node structure for binary tree */
struct bin_node
    {
    hold_t           *element;    /* data held in node */
    struct bin_node *left;        /* left child node */
    struct bin_node *right;       /* right child node */
    struct bin_node *parent;       /* parent node */
    };

typedef struct bin_node bin_t;
```

In this structure definition, the data type hold_t is a predefined structure that holds the information you want stored in the node. This structure is like info_t, which is used for linked lists.

Note that a pointer to the parent node is included. This pointer, like the doubly linked list's prev pointer, is convenient for "backing up" in a tree. Space for one pointer for each element is a small price to pay for greater flexibility, which is needed for many applications. You also can use NULL pointers. If, for example, a binary tree node has no left child, that node's left pointer has the value NULL.

The preceding structure definition can be extended for trees that have more than two child nodes. For example, if the maximum is three children, you can use

```
/* node structure for three children per node */
struct tri_node
    {
    hold_t          *element;
    struct tri_node *left;
    struct tri_node *middle;
    struct tri_node *right;
    struct tri_node *parent;
    };

typedef struct tri_node tri_t;
```

For more than three child nodes, an array of child nodes is convenient. This array can be constructed with an array of pointers to the child nodes, as follows:

```
/* node structure for fixed number of children (MAX) */
struct ary_node
    {
    hold_t          *element;       /* data in node */
    struct ary_node *child[MAX];    /* array of child nodes */
    struct ary_node *parent;        /* parent node */
    };

typedef struct ary_node ary_t;
```

Trees with a Variable Number of Child Nodes

This last structure gives the clue as to how to construct a structure to handle a general-purpose tree in which the number of child nodes cannot be predicted at compile time. The array of child nodes is replaced by a linked list of children. This method has two advantages. The number of child nodes can grow to any size, and the program does not allocate unneeded memory. Each node in the linked list of children, of course, contains a pointer to another general tree structure. You can apply all the functions developed in Chapter 5 to this application by designating `info_t` as the name of the data type for general trees, as follows:

```
/* node structure for an arbitrary number of children */
struct info
    {
    hold_t      *element;        /* data in node */
    struct head *children;       /* linked list of children */
    struct info *parent;         /* parent node */
    };


typedef struct info info_t;
```

The preceding definition should be studied carefully (see fig. 6.7). Each node of the tree (which is type `info_t`) is composed of three pointers. The first (`element`) points to information to be associated with the node. The second (`children`) points to a linked list of child nodes of that node. This linked list is composed of a head of type `head_t` followed by a list of nodes, each of which can contain a pointer to another tree node. By choosing the name of the data type for tree nodes to be `info_t`, the data type used for data stored in the nodes of a list, you can use, without any modifications, all of the previously developed list manipulation functions for operating on the list of child nodes. This will save a great deal of effort when constructing the tree manipulation functions. The example uses a singly linked list, but a doubly linked list can be used if the application requires more complex relationships among the child nodes. Finally, the tree node contains a pointer to its parent, which again is a tree node, and so type `info_t`. For simplicity, the pointers contained within the parent and child nodes are not shown in the figure.

In the case of trees, a separate header node is not particularly useful. With all the information present in each node, the nodes themselves act as miniheaders for the the subtrees. You need to maintain only an `info_t` pointer variable that contains the starting address of a tree.

Operations on Trees

As for linked lists, a set of functions to perform generally useful actions on trees is convenient. Many of these functions make extensive use of the data types and list manipulation functions

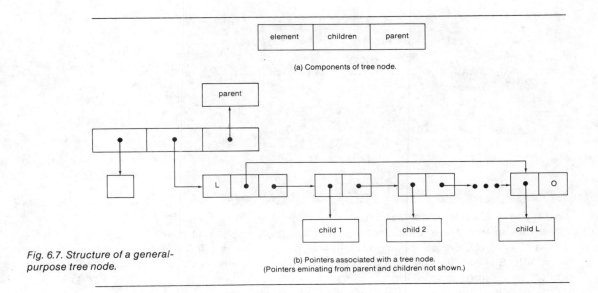

(a) Components of tree node.

Fig. 6.7. Structure of a general-purpose tree node.

(b) Pointers associated with a tree node.
(Pointers eminating from parent and children not shown.)

discussed in Chapter 5. Therefore, a file containing these tree functions also should include the appropriate linked list structure and function definitions. (These definitions can be in the same file or in another file and brought in by means of #include.)

Instantiating a New Tree Node

Because you are not using a header for trees, you have no counterpart to the create function that you used for linked lists. However, you do have a tree node instantiation function, which appears as follows:

```
/* instantiate a new tree node */
info_t  *inst_info(data, parent)
hold_t  *data;
info_t  *parent;
{
    info_t  *new;
    head_t  *create();

    /* attempt allocation and initialization */
    if (new = MALLOC(info_t))
```

```
        {
        /* allocation OK, proceed with initialization */
        new->element = data;
        /* attempt creation of new list of children */
        if ((new->children = create()) == NULL)
            return(NULL);
        new->parent = parent;
        }


    /* done */
    return(new);
}
```

Two types of allocation are used in this function. Memory is provided for the tree node itself, and the initially empty list of child nodes is created. For simplicity, these two operations are combined into a single function. Note that the value of the children pointer is obtained by making a call to the create function. This function, defined in chapter 5, creates a new linked list (the list of child nodes, in this case) and returns a pointer to the list's header. This newly created list, of course, consists only of the header itself. Therefore, if a tree node exists, you can be sure that its children pointer also has been set to some value that is not NULL.

You can then write a simple function that puts the first (the root) node in a new tree:

```
/*
    start a new tree
    returns address of root node
*/
info_t  *init_tree(data)
hold_t  *data;
{
    info_t  *inst_info();

    return(inst_info(data, NULL));
}
```

Note that the function returns a pointer to the root node.

Adding Nodes

Next, you need a routine that adds a child node to another node. This operation may create a new level in the hierarchy by adding a child to a leaf node (see fig. 6.8), or the operation simply may increase the number of child nodes for a nonleaf node that already has one or more children (see fig. 6.9). In either case, the function is simple to construct. After making a call to the instantiation routine, the function invokes the previously defined **append** function (see Chapter 5), which adds a new element to the current list of children. If you are adding a child to a leaf node, that node's current list of children has a header but no other elements. If you are adding a child to a nonleaf node, the current list of children consists of a header and one or more elements. The **append** function works properly in either situation. The code for this operation follows.

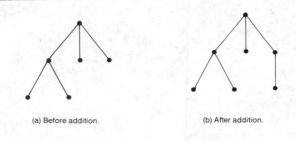

(a) Before addition.   (b) After addition.

Fig. 6.8. Adding a child to a leaf node.

Fig. 6.9. Adding a child to a nonleaf node.

```
/*
   add a child to any tree node
   assumes argument t_node is not NULL
*/
BOOLEAN add_child(data, t_node)
hold_t  *data;
info_t  *t_node;
{
    info_t  *new, *inst_info();
    BOOLEAN append();
```

```
    /* attempt instantiation */
    if (new = inst_info(data, t_node))
        /* link new node into list of children */
        return(append(new, t_node->children));

    /* instantiation failed */
    return(FALSE);
}
```

Similarly, you may want to add a new sibling to a list of child nodes. This operation can be accomplished by making a call to the previous add_child function, as follows:

```
/*
    add a sibling to any tree node (except the root)
    assumes argument t_node->parent is not NULL
*/
BOOLEAN add_sibl(data, t_node)
hold_t *data;
info_t *t_node;
{
    BOOLEAN add_child();

    /* link new node into parent's list of children */
    return(add_child(data, t_node->parent));
}
```

As the comment states, the only problem occurs if you try to add a sibling to the root of a tree. Therefore, before invoking this function, the application must check the value of t_node->parent to confirm that the value is not NULL. (The root is the only node of a tree whose parent is NULL.)

Traversing Trees

Next, consider a function that is useful in traversing the nodes of a tree. This function returns a pointer to the leftmost child (the first child) of a parent node. Note that the return value is defined as a node_t pointer rather than an info_t pointer. (Recall that in the examples in Chapter 5, node_t is the data type used for the nodes of a linked list.) This definition gives you access to the next pointer, which indicates where the other child nodes are.

```
/*
    find the leftmost child of a tree node
    assumes argument t_node is not NULL
    returns pointer to type node_t
*/
node_t  *leftmost(t_node)
info_t  *t_node;
{
    return(t_node->children->first);
}
```

If you make a call like

```
node_t  *ptr, leftmost();
info_t  *tree;

...

ptr = leftmost(tree);
```

the leftmost child node is in ptr->item, and the next child in the list (called the *right sibling*) is found at ptr->next.

If one application contains several trees, you may need to find the root of a tree when the program is given a pointer to any of that tree's nodes. To find the root, have the program follow the series of parent pointers until the program reaches a NULL value, which indicates that the root has been found. This operation is illustrated in the following code lines:

```
/*
    find the root of a tree, given any node
    assumes argument t_node is not NULL
*/
info_t  *root(t_node)
info_t  *t_node;
{
    /* search for NULL parent */
    while (t_node->parent)
        t_node = t_node->parent;

    /* found the root */
    return(t_node);
}
```

To be able to tell whether a given node is a leaf node is also convenient. This capability simply requires an examination of the
length of the linked list of the node's children.

```
/*
    is node a leaf node?
    assumes argument t_node is not NULL
*/
BOOLEAN is_leaf(t_node)
info_t *t_node;
{
    /* any child nodes? */
    if (t_node->children->length)    /* yes => not a leaf */
        return(FALSE);
    else                             /* no => is a leaf */
        return(TRUE);
}
```

Finally, consider functions that perform a complete traversal of a
tree. Each function uses one of the three methods discussed:
preorder, in-order, or postorder. While traversing the tree, the application may carry out a specified operation on each node. This
operation may be as simple as printing the node's contents, or it
may involve something more complex. The following three functions are based on the assumption that the user has defined a
function do_it to perform a designated operation on each tree
node.

```
/*
    perform preorder traversal of tree
    assumes function do_it exists
    assumes argument t_node is not NULL
*/
void    pre_ord(t_node)
info_t *t_node;
{

    node_t *temp, leftmost();
    void    do_it();

    /* first take root node itself */
    do_it(t_node);
```

```
    /* then take children (if any) in left-to-right order */
    if (t_node->children->length)
        {
        temp = leftmost(t_node);
        while (temp)
            {
            pre_ord(temp->item);
            temp = temp->next;
            }
        }
}

/*
   perform in-order traversal of tree
   assumes function do_it exists
   assumes argument t_node is not NULL
*/
void      in_ord(t_node)
info_t  *t_node;
{
    node_t   *temp, leftmost();
    void     do_it();

    if (t_node->children->length == 0)   /* trivial case */
        do_it(t_node);
    else                                 /* nontrivial case */
        {
        temp = leftmost(t_node);
        in_ord(temp->item);
        do_it(t_node);
        temp = temp->next;
        while(temp)
            {
            in_ord(temp->item);
            temp = temp->next;
            }
        }
}
```

```
/*
   perform postorder traversal of tree
   assumes function do_it exists
   assumes argument t_node is not NULL
*/
void    post_ord(t_node)
info_t  *t_node;
{
    node_t  *temp, leftmost();
    void    do_it();

    /* first take children (if any) in left-to-right order */
    if (t_node->children->length)
        {
        temp = leftmost(t_node);
        while (temp)
            {
            post_ord(temp->item);
            temp = temp->next;
                }
            }

    /* then take root node itself */
    do_it(t_node);
}
```

Many other functions can be defined for manipulating trees. The functions explained in this chapter can guide you in constructing other functions.

Forests

You can create more complex associations of data by using combinations of trees. A collection of trees is usually referred to as a *forest*.

The simplest method to build a forest is to build an array of trees. For example,

```
/* number of trees in forest */
#define FOR_SIZE    10

/* array of pointers to trees */
info_t  *fst_1[FOR_SIZE];
```

You also may choose to build a forest by using one of the types of linked lists discussed in Chapter 5. You may have singly or doubly linked lists of trees, a stack of trees, or a queue of trees. However, you must be careful to separate the two kinds of linked lists in the data structure: the list of the trees themselves and the linked lists that are embedded within each tree node to hold the children of that node. Because these lists are constructed from different types of elements, you must separate the data types.

Consider, for example, a forest constructed from a linked list of trees. You can define new data types for the forest as follows:

```
/* node for linked list of trees */
struct fst_node
    {
    info_t      *fst_item;
    struct node *fst_next;
    };

typedef struct fst_node fst_n_t;

/* header for linked list of trees */
struct fst_head
    {
    int     fst_len;
    fst_n_t *fst_first, *fst_last;
    };

typedef struct fst_head fst_h_t;
```

You can define a pointer to a forest of this type by writing

```
fst_h_t *fst_2;      /* pointer to linked list of trees */
```

The only remaining task is to define new routines to manipulate the linked list of trees, which are routines you already have defined. The only difference is that the names of the data types must be changed to the two names given: fst_n_t and fst_h_t. The functionality is unchanged. A doubly linked list, stack, and queue of trees can be defined and manipulated similarly.

In this chapter and the preceding one, you have seen how to construct new data types and a set of operations on those types. The C concepts of pointers and structures have played a central role in these two chapters, allowing complex associations of data to be created and manipulated as a program is executing.

The final three chapters contain detailed examples of how data types and their associated operations actually are used in practice. The graphics system and advanced user interface to be presented next are illustrations of the power and flexibility that C can provide.

7

Application Graphics

Several approaches to graphics are available in C, but some methods present problems. For instance, most computer systems allow in-line graphics calls to system-dependent functions. This approach, however, results in an application that is difficult, if not impossible, to transport to other environments. On systems that support a graphics standard, such as CORE or GKS, the C programmer can use header files to access the graphics functions and include these standard calls in the application code. Graphics standards appear to solve all problems, but they are actually a double-edged sword. Because these standards are available on only a few mature computer systems, the portability of applications using these standards is limited. In addition, most graphics standards are implemented in a language other than C, usually FORTRAN. This fact may cause interface problems between application variables and graphics variables. Standards, because of their generality, require large amounts of memory, which prohibits their use on smaller computers. (The full CORE standard is more than 200K bytes!) Graphics standards, therefore, address the needs of the C programmer only at a considerable cost.

An attractive alternative to using a graphics standard is to create standards written in C. You can define a C graphics library similar to the C function library. A graphics library and the function library have the same advantages: a common interface and transportability. This chapter describes a C graphics library and provides the basis for the advanced user interface discussed in Chapters 8 and 9. The program code for the segmentation system presented in this chapter is in Appendix A.

Introduction to Graphics Systems

Application graphics is fast becoming a standard and necessary information display technique. The way in which large quantities of information are presented often determines the success or failure of a program. The old proverb "A picture is worth a thousand words" is as true for computer systems as for other mediums. For example, a geological survey contains many data samples that represent the contours of a piece of land. Each data sample consists of a location and an altitude. Several methods are available for presenting this information (such as large tables of numbers), but pictures show best what has been measured. By processing the data samples and displaying them as a contour map, you can immediately present the complete results of the survey. If you allow the user to interact with the contour map by displaying specific altitudes or by viewing smaller areas of the map, the usefulness of the application increases even more.

Pictures are the output of a graphics system; but how are they generated? Consider again the preceding example. To present data interactively, you must first decide how the data is to be represented. Each data point in the survey has a distinct location, which you can transform into a point on your display. For each location, you can assign a specific color, perhaps according to the altitude. The resulting image consists of many colored points, each representative of the data sampled. Another approach links points of equal altitude with lines to form a contour map. Yet another way to present the data is to form regions of equal altitude into polygons and fill the polygons with the corresponding colors.

Whatever method you choose, you must model the data in some intermediate form before you can display it. While graphics systems do not understand geological surveys, they do understand things like points, lines, polygons, text, and circles. These modeling elements, called *primitives*, are the simplest elements. All images are constructed from primitives.

With each graphical primitive, you associate modifying parameters, such as patterns and colors. This parameter information can be included with each primitive. With so many types of parameters, however, this practice wastes storage; and if you must reset the display parameters for every primitive, the execution speed of the graphics system is greatly reduced. A better way of describing parameters is through another modeling element called an *attribute*. Attributes modify the way in which primitives are displayed, and attributes must be defined before primitives in the application code in the drawing process. The underlying concept is that the display of primitives can be predetermined. For instance, the line-drawing color may be set to green. From that point on, all lines are drawn in green. Similarly, you may set another attribute so that all primitives are filled in and appear solid. These attribute states remain in effect until individually changed. For most applications, use of attributes results in greater economy of the information required to display complex images.

Before you can describe a primitive, you must decide on a coordinate system. A common approach uses a two-dimensional Cartesian model, with x increasing to the right and y increasing upward. Two variable types are available for representing coordinates: integers and floating-point numbers. Integers, as fixed-point numbers, allow only limited element resolution but offer relatively fast execution. Because computer displays also are limited in resolution, integers (or longs) do not pose a problem in most sit-uations. Floating-point numbers offer much better resolution, but the C specification requiring that all floating-point mathematics be performed with double precision is costly in terms of execution speed. (Floating-point variables are useful in situations that involve scaling integers by arbitrary amounts.) Without specialized acceleration hardware for floating-point mathematics, an interactive graphics application must be restricted to an integer representation. The following explanation uses integer variables for all coordinates.

Throughout this section, the word *display* is used generically. The computerized generation of an image can be performed by means of several different hardware devices, but the most common viewing device is the *raster*, or *bit-mapped display*. An example of this type of display is a television monitor coupled to display hardware like that found in a personal computer. Other graphical display devices create images on paper or plastic. These devices include all forms of plotters and printers, which often are used to create hardcopy images of raster displays.

Obviously, an interactive application requires a dynamic (continually updatable) display. This limitation effectively reduces the choice of output device to the raster display. However, because raster displays are common, this limitation is not at all severe. Assume the use of a bit-mapped raster display for all the examples in the rest of this book.

An Introduction to Segmentation

The earlier chapters describe a method for large-program development. The basic strategy consists of combining logically related subroutines and variables into individual files. These code segments can be compiled separately and later linked to form the program. This programming style encourages clear organization, short compile times, and manageable maintenance of large applications. In many ways, methods for graphical element description and manipulation are similar to this development style. By grouping related graphical elements into segments (the graphics counterpart of files), you can describe and manipulate images with minimum effort and maximum effectiveness. This section shows how segments are created and used to construct composite images.

Images are constructed by using graphical primitives with attributes that modify the display of those primitives. Primitives and attributes can be considered graphical commands, because a sequence of these commands causes the application to form an image. When describing graphical elements, you often can form groups of commands that are common to some or to all the elements. By putting these logically related commands in segments, you can treat a group of commands as a single element. A segment can be manipulated and viewed as if it were a single entity. Segments also can refer to other segments in a hierarchical description of images. This referencing operation is known as *instancing*, because an instance of one segment is included inside another.

Creating Segments

Segments are constructed in much the same manner as disk files. First, you create the segment. Then information (graphical commands) is added to the segment. Finally, the segment is closed. So that you can use the segment, the routine that closes the segment returns a pointer to it. An outline of the code for this operation could be written as

```
CREATE_SEGMENT(segment_name);

    /* add image information */
    ATTRIBUTE(...);
    PRIMITIVE(...);
    INSTANCE(...);

    ...
segment_pointer = CLOSE_SEGMENT();
```

Note: In this section of the book, capital letters represent generic graphics operations. Using generic functions, the basic concepts can be explained simply and clearly. These are not the implemented functions, but rather a form of "pseudocode" that clearly describes what actions must be taken in order to create the segments. Later sections show how the functions actually are implemented in C code.

A simple example of segmentation is the graphical description of a city block consisting of four identical houses (see fig. 7.1). Each house has three windows, a door, and the framework. First, create segments for the window and door.

```
/* declare pointers to segments */
segment_t  *window, *door, *house, *block;

CREATE_SEGMENT( "window" );

    ATTRIBUTE(BLUE);
    RECTANGLE( 10, 10, 60, 80);
    RECTANGLE( 10,  0, 60, 90);

window = CLOSE_SEGMENT();

CREATE_SEGMENT( "door" );

    ATTRIBUTE(CYAN);
    RECTANGLE( 0,  0, 50, 100);

door = CLOSE_SEGMENT();
```

When a segment is created, all of its attributes are assumed to be set to a black background and a draw color (for all primitives) of white. Primitives with nonzero area (that is, everything other than points and lines) are not "filled in" but *framed;* that is, you draw a border along the perimeters.

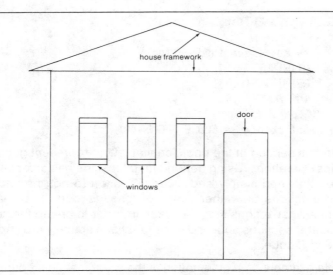

Fig. 7.1. The house.

You next create the house segment, which instances the window and the door segments.

```
CREATE_SEGMENT( "house" );

    ATTRIBUTE(YELLOW);
    RECT( 100, 100, 600, 500);

    /* add a line for the roof */
    BEGIN_LINE();
        CONTINUE_POINT( 50,   480);
        CONTINUE_POINT( 350, 600);
        CONTINUE_POINT( 650, 480);
    ADD_LINE( END_LINE() );

    /* instance windows and door */
    INSTANCE( "window", 150, 300);
    INSTANCE( "window", 250, 300);
    INSTANCE( "window", 350, 300);
    INSTANCE( "door",   450, 100);

    house = CLOSE_SEGMENT();
```

Note the format of the instance command. The segment name and relative position, or offset, describe the instance. The instanced segments are offset from the origin of the house segment by the specified x and y amounts. This simple feature makes instancing a powerful command that allows a hierarchical representation of graphical data. Also, note that a segment pointer to the instance command is not supplied. The instance command assumes that the given segment will exist when the instancing segment is drawn. This allows you to create segments in any order, as long as all segments exist when they are needed by the segmentation system. Therefore, you can instance segments that have not been created yet.

The final step is to create the city-block segment, which instances the house segment.

```
CREATE_SEGMENT( "block" );

     INSTANCE( "house", 0,    0);
     INSTANCE( "house", 800,  0);
     INSTANCE( "house", 1600, 0);
     INSTANCE( "house", 2400, 0);

block = CLOSE_SEGMENT();
```

Note the hierarchical structure of this example. The city block contains houses, which, in turn, contain windows and doors. If you do not use a hierarchical method for describing the city block, you have to code separately twelve windows, four doors, and four house frames. However, by using a hierarchical approach, you create each element only once. To update an element in your design—for example, to add curtains to the windows—you update only the one window segment. All future instances to the updated segment reflect the change.

Using Segments

To view the results of any or of all the segments just created, you simply initialize your display and make the call

```
DRAW_SEGMENT( segment_pointer );
```

Note that the segment-draw routine uses a segment pointer rather than the segment's name. Because the program does not have to search a list of segment names to find the right segment, this practice provides the maximum possible drawing speed. You also can define a function that, given a segment name, returns a pointer to that segment. This function looks like

```
segment_pointer *GET_SEG_PTR( segment_name ) ;
```

You often need to save segments in files. A graphical segment stored in a disk file, called a *graphics metafile*, provides a method for graphical resource storage. Metafiles can be instanced from segments currently in main memory and from other metafiles. When an instance of a segment is not in main memory, the graphics system searches the disk for a metafile with a name that matches the specified instance. If the matching metafile is found, the graphics system reads that metafile into a segment.

With metafiles, an application can use many more segments than the system has memory to accommodate. If an application has used all the main memory and needs more, the application determines which segments can be written to a metafile and deleted from memory. If a segment is to be used every time an application is run, simply reading a metafile from the disk is far more sensible than recreating the segment each time it is needed.

The system outlined supports hierarchical modeling of graphical data. Based on graphics primitives and attributes, this system provides the means for building a powerful graphics library from which to construct applications. The library has all the features inherent in the C language, including an efficient, compact, modular code and a high degree of transportability among computer systems. With this tool, applications developers can increase their productivity significantly. The remainder of this chapter describes in greater detail the data structures and the functions that make up this graphics library.

The Graphical Segmentation System

In this section, the collection of C data structures and functions that form the graphical segmentation system are explained. However, this section presents only the interface to the segmentation system. The actual C code that implements the complete system is presented Appendix A.

Primitives

The lowest-level graphical elements in the segmentation system are the primitives and their associated operators. A few commonly used primitives are given in this text, and you can easily add more primitives to the system. Each primitive has a C data structure and a set of associated C functions that create, draw, and insert the primitive in the open segment. You also are given routines that operate on all primitives. These routines read and write files, determine certain properties of primitives, and free primitives from dynamic memory.

The Point

The simplest primitive is the point. Following the style presented in earlier chapters, the C structure for the point is

```
struct point_primitive
    {
    int x,  y;
    };

typedef struct point_primitive point_t;
```

To create a point, use the following function call. The (x, y) location of the point is passed to the function call, which returns a pointer to the newly-allocated point structure.

```
point_t *inst_point( x,  y )
```

The Rectangle

The next primitive is the rectangle. This primitive describes a graphical element that is used to represent all rectangular regions, such as bit maps and viewports. The C structure for the rectangle is

```
struct rect_primitive
    {
    int left,  bottom,  right,  top;
    };

typedef struct rect_primitive rect_t;
```

To create a rectangle, use the following function call. The coordinates of the rectangle are passed to the function call, which returns a pointer to the newly allocated rectangle structure.

```
rect_t    *inst_rect( left,  bottom,  right,  top )
```

Rectangles are useful for describing the bounding boxes of both primitives and segments. A *bounding box* is simply a rectangular region that encloses the total x,y area of the rectangle's associated graphical element. Bounding boxes are used to determine whether a graphical element is viewable, that is, whether any part of the element is to be considered for drawing on the display. For these and many other graphical operations, a set of utility routines has been defined to operate on rectangles and points. The routines are

```
#define TRUE   1
#define FALSE  0
#define BOOLEAN int /* TRUE or FALSE */

/* point or x,y location within rectangle */
BOOLEAN pt_in_rect( rect_pointer, point_pointer )
BOOLEAN loc_in_rect( rect_pointer, x, y )

/* intersection operation, C set to result */
BOOLEAN sect_rect( rect_pointer_A, rect_pointer_B, rect_pointer_C )

/* union operation, C set to result */
union_rect( rect_pointer_A, rect_pointer_B, rect_pointer_C )

/* rectangle move and resize operations */
rect_t  *offset_rect( rect_pointer, delta_h, delta_v )
rect_t  *inset_rect( rect_pointer, delta_h, delta_v )

/* rectangle reset and copy operation */
rect_t  *set_rect( left, bottom, right, top )
rect_t  *copy_rect( old_rect_pointer );
```

The Oval

The next primitive to be considered has the same data structure as the rectangle, but describes ovals. In this case, the rectangle defines the bounding box of the oval. If the rectangle is a square, the oval is a circle. By taking advantage of the previously defined rectangle structures and functions, you need to define only the following:

```
#define  oval_t   rect_t
#define  inst_oval  inst_rect
```

Of course, you still have separate functions for drawing rectangles and ovals.

The Multipoint Line and the Polygon

The next two primitives, the multipoint line and the polygon, are variable in size. The data structures for these two primitives are identical. However, in some situations, you may want to modify one or both, such as by adding a width variable to the line primitive. To allow for alterations, define these primitives separately.

Because these two primitives are variable in length, linked lists are used to gain efficiency and flexibility (see chapter 5). Each primitive consists of a head part and a list of nodes. To implement the list of nodes, use a data structure called a *continue point*, which consists of the point structure and a pointer to the next continue point. During the traversal of this list, when you find a next pointer that is NULL, you have come to the end of the linked list. The continue point data structure is defined as follows:

```
struct    cont_point
    {
    point_t point;
    struct  cont_point  *next;
    };

    typedef struct cont_point cpoint_t;
```

The data structures for the line and polygon can be defined in terms of this structure:

```
struct line_primitive
    {
    int      num_points;
    rect_t   *bbox;
    struct   cpoint_t   *point;
    };

    typedef struct line_primitive line_t;
```

```
struct poly_primitive
    {
    int     num_points;
    rect_t  *bbox;
    struct  cpoint_t    *point;
    };
```

```
typedef struct poly_primitive poly_t;
```

In these two definitions, bbox is a pointer to the rectangular bounding box for the line or the polygon. To create a line primitive, first call the routine begin_line(). Then add continue points with successive calls to con_point() in order to construct the line of the polygon. Finally, call end_line(), which returns a pointer to the newly created line structure. An example of this process, which creates a line from coordinates 1 to N, is

```
/* declare line pointers */
line_t  *myline, *end_line();

begin_line();
    con_point( x1, y1 );
    con_point( x2, y2 );
    . . .
    con_point( xN, yN );
myline = end_line();
```

Polygon primitives are created in exactly the same manner, except that polygons are closed (that is, polygons have an "inside" and an "outside"). Specifying the final line segment that closes the polygon is superfluous because polygon routines employ a convenient shorthand to close the figures. If the last point of the polygon (at the end of the polygon description) does not match the first point, a new point is added automatically to close the polygon. An example of a polygon creation is

```
/* declare polygon pointers */
poly_t  *mypoly, *end_poly();

begin_poly();
    con_point( x1, y1 );
    con_point( x2, y2 );
    . . .
    con_point( xN, yN );
mypoly = end_poly();
```

The Text Primitive

The last primitive in the set stores text. Many computer systems operate in either a text only mode or a graphics only mode, and so cannot support graphics and text at the same time. However, with a little ingenuity (and a lot of memory!), you can implement text on any graphics system by using the line primitive to form each text character individually. (Text fonts that are based on line segments are called stroke fonts.) The following text primitive is included for users who are able to implement text within graphics on their systems.

The text primitive uses a technique called *justification*. With justification you can modify the direction that the text string is drawn from its origin. For example, to place a set of text primitives so that the centers of the text strings are aligned, set the origins of each primitive at the same horizontal coordinate and set the horizontal justification of each primitive at MIDDLE. The following examples show the kinds of horizontal justification.

This	This	This
is	is	is
left	middle	right
justification	justification	justification

The C justification definitions and data structure for the text primitive are

```
/*

        text justification definitions
```

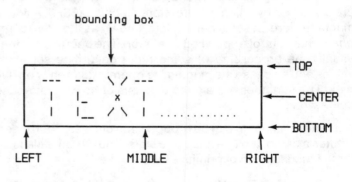

```
*/
```

```
#define TOP      't'
#define CENTER   'c'
#define BOTTOM   'b'
#define LEFT     'l'
#define MIDDLE   'm'
#define RIGHT    'r'
#define TXTSZE   32

struct  text_primitive
    {
    point_t origin;
    rect_t *bbox;        /* bounding box  */
    char    just[2];     /* justification: [0] => x, [1] => y */
    char    text[TXTSZE];
    };

typedef struct  text_primitive  text_t;
```

To create a text primitive, you must call an instantiation function, to which are passed a pointer to a text string, the location of the primitive, and both horizontal and vertical justification constants. The function returns a pointer to the newly allocated primitive. This instantiation function call is

```
text_t *inst_text( char_pointer, x, y, jh, jv )
```

Attributes

Attributes are graphical operators that modify the way primitives are displayed by using a *finite-state machine (FSM)*. A finite-state machine stores a set of parameters, known as the *state of the machine*, that control a specified operation. The operation of the FSM, usually the processing of some input data, may set new state values and so cause the machine to operate differently on different data. The attributes are a good example of how a finite-state machine works.

Attribute commands can be grouped into classes. Each class constitutes a part of the total machine state. The attribute classes used for the modification of primitives are:

```
bit map draw mode       /* how pixels are added to the  display */
bit map draw color      /* the value of the added pixel */
primitive fill mode     /* fill with current color */
primitive frame mode    /* outline with current color */
```

For each class, declare an integer variable to hold the current attribute of that class. The values of the attributes can be encoded conveniently by a set of constants. These defined constants will be available (from an include file) to all functions that may require access to the values of the attributes. In addition, you can add a reset command, which, when passed to the FSM, sets the machine to a predefined state. The encodings of the attributes, in order of the classes listed in the last paragraph, are:

```
/* bit map draw modes */
#define COPY      10
#define XOR       11

/* bit map draw colors */
#define BLACK     20
#define RED       21
#define GREEN     22
#define BLUE      23
#define CYAN      24
#define MAGENTA 25
#define YELLOW  26
#define WHITE    27

/* primitive fill modes */
#define FILL      12
#define NOFILL   13

/* primitive frame modes */
#define FRAME     14
#define NOFRAME 15

/* FSM reset command */
#define RESET    99
```

Note the numbering scheme of the attribute definitions. The selection of these constants is purely arbitrary, but you should allow for future expansion of both the attribute classes and the commands. The reset state for the FSM in this text is draw mode, copy; color, white; primitives, do not fill; and primitives, frame. The code for this attribute-driven FSM is sketched as follows:

```
/* declare the class state variables */
int  draw_mode, draw_color, fill_mode, frame_mode;
```

```
/* entry point to FSM */
switch(attribute)
    {
    /* RESET STATE COMMAND */
    case    RESET   :
        draw_mode  = COPY;
        draw_color = WHITE;
        fill_mode  = NOFILL;
        frame_mode = FRAME;
        break;

    /* CLASS: DRAW MODE */
    case    COPY    :
    case    XOR     :
        draw_mode = attribute;
        break;

    /* CLASS: DRAW COLOR */
    case    BLACK   :
    case    RED     :
    case    GREEN   :
    case    BLUE    :
    case    CYAN    :
    case    MAGENTA :
    case    YELLOW  :
    case    WHITE   :
        draw_color = attribute;
        break;

    /* CLASS: FILL MODE */
    case    FILL    :
    case    NOFILL  :
        file_mode = attribute;
        break;

    /* CLASS: FRAME MODE */
    case    FRAME   :
    case    NOFRAME :
        frame_mode = attribute;
        break;
```

```
/* insert additional attribute classes here */

default :
    error("Unknown attribute");
}
/* end of FSM */
```

Segment Operations

Segments, as shown throughout this chapter, are the basis for the power and flexibility of this graphics system. As the primary modeling elements in the system, segments hold both attributes and primitives. Because segments are variable-length data structures, the linked list concepts are appropriate for segment descriptions. Each segment consists of a head part and a list of elements called *keys*. Each key holds an attribute or a primitive. Individual segments are stored in a linked list of segments so that you can work with many segments at once. The segment head is defined to be

```
struct  segment
    {
    int     num_inst, visible, locked;
    char    *name;
    rect_t  *bbox;
    key_t   *data,
            *eol;
    struct  segment *next;
    };

typedef struct segment seg_t;
```

Several important data fields should be noted in this structure definition. Because a segment may be instanced by other segments through the reference command, you must keep track of exactly how many instances to each segment are in effect at any given moment. If you delete from memory a segment that has been instanced by another segment and try to redraw the instancing segment, you soon will find corrupted variables, and imminent doom awaits. Use the num_inst variable to track the number of instances made to each segment. The variable visible turns off the display of a segment without deleting it. The variable locked prevents a segment from ever being deleted from memory by setting the segment's value to TRUE. The name and bbox variables are pointers, respectively, to a character string and the bounding box of the

segment. The next two variables, data and eol, are pointers, respectively, to the beginning and end of the linked list of graphical
commands that make up the segment. Finally, you define the variable next, which points to the next segment in a list of segments.
What you actually have is a list of lists: you have a list of segments
that make up an image, and each segment, in turn, is a list of primitive and attribute graphics commands.

Defining the Nodes

Because the nodes of a segment list (the keys) can hold several
different types of primitives and attributes, use the variant-record
structure to define the nodes. Recall that this kind of structure is
composed of two parts. First, a simple integer variable keeps track
of the type of element stored in the node. Second, a union is defined to hold one of the several possible graphics primitives. To
use this structure as a list node, also add a pointer to the next element in the list. The type definitions and C data structure for the
keys are

```
/* Key primitive types */
#define POINT   1
#define LINE    2
#define RECT    3
#define POLY    4
#define OVAL    5
#define TEXT    6
#define REF     7
/* add your primitives here */

struct  seg_key
    {
    int type;
    union   /* of all possible primitives */
        {
        char    *ptr;
        point_t *point;
        line_t  *line;
        rect_t  *rect;
        poly_t  *poly;
        oval_t  *oval;
        text_t  *text;
        ref_t   *ref;
        } key;
```

```
struct  seg_key *next;
};
```

```
typedef struct  seg_key key_t;
```

Note that a character pointer is included in the key's union field. With this pointer, you can assign primitive pointers to the key by using a single generic routine. In effect, with this feature, you can assign a pointer to the key without having to know the type of data structure to which the pointer points.

To store an attribute command within the key structure, do not use the union field. Only the type variable describes an attribute command. For example, if a key is to hold the attribute that fills primitives, the type field is set to the defined constant FILL, and the union field key is ignored.

Creating a Segment

To create a segment, define only a pointer that points to the segment; then make a call to the function cr_seg(). This function creates a new segment structure, links it to the current list of segments, and NULLs the pointers that construct the segment's key list. To add attribute and primitive commands to the segment, call only the function append(type, pointer). The type field of the append function is one of the predefined attribute or primitive types. The pointer field is a pointer to the primitive that is to be appended to the segment. If an attribute is to be appended to the segment, the pointer field is ignored. Primitives are drawn on the display in the order in which they are appended to the segment list. To complete the construction of a segment, call the function cl_seg(). This function terminates the construction of the segment by assigning the remaining pointers for the linked list of keys, calculating the bounding box of the segment, declaring the segment to be visible and unlocked, and returning a pointer to the segment.

Opening and Closing a Segment

You can open a previously created (and closed) segment and append graphical commands to it. Open the segment with the function op_seg(segment_pointer). Close an opened segment performs all the operations described in the preceding paragraph, including the recalculation of the segment's bounding box.

Deleting a Segment

The next segment operation deletes a segment. This function takes the form del_seg(segment_pointer). The delete operation first checks to see whether the segment is unlocked and not instanced by another segment. If these two conditions are met, the segment's list of keys is removed (freed) from memory, and the segment structure itself is removed.

Making a Reference to a Segment

By placing an instance of an element inside another, you obtain the hierarchical nature of the graphical modeling system. This kind of operation is referred to as a reference. A *reference* to a segment is made through a data structure that stores the necessary information about the instance. This structure is defined as

```
struct  reference
    {
    point_t origin;
    seg_t   *instance;
    char    name[TXTSZE];
    };

    typedef struct  reference   ref_t;
```

The origin field of the reference structure is the distance of the offset that the instanced segment is to be drawn from the current segment. The instance variable points to a segment structure. If this pointer is NULL, a metafile must exist from which to read the instanced segment. The name variable is the instanced segment's name (as defined by the application) or a graphics metafile name. To create a reference, call the function

```
    ref_t  *inst_ref( name, x, y,  segment_name )
```

The preceding function is passed a segment (or metafile) name, the offset of the segment, and an optional pointer. By supplying a pointer to a known segment, you can eliminate the search through the list of segments for the instanced segment. If no pointer is supplied to this function, the calling function should supply a NULL pointer. If no pointer is specified, the instantiation function uses whatever value is on the system's stack—an action that usually causes a fatal error.

Creating and Retrieving Metafiles

Creating and retrieving metafiles are simple routines. To write a segment to a metafile, call the function `wr_seg( segment_pointer )`. To read a segment from a metafile, call `rd_seg( segment_name )`. The latter function takes a character string as its argument and returns a pointer to the newly created segment.

The read-metafile routine has some "smarts." The program first checks the list of segments in memory to see whether the requested segment exists. If the segment does exist, a pointer to that segment is returned. If an instanced segment is not in memory when its referencing segment is drawn, the draw function attempts to read the instanced metafile from the disk.

Geometrical Transformations

The descriptions of primitives, attributes, and segments refer to certain drawing operations that transform a graphical model to an image on a display. In the examples, a single segment, which fills the entire display, is visible. These examples, of course, give an overly simplistic view of the required transformation from model to display.

Viewing several segments at once, each in its own section of the display, is possible and often desirable. Also, to get a closer look at some area or item, you may enlarge specific sections of a segment. These operations are performed by geometrical transformations.

To understand the transformation of a graphical model into a displayed image, you must first understand two coordinate systems: world coordinates and display coordinates. *World coordinates* are the integers used to describe graphical primitives. *Display coordinates*, on the other hand, correspond to the pixels ("picture elements") in the raster display where you actually place the graphical image.

Defining Windows

To describe in world coordinates the geometrical data you wish transformed into an image, you must define a window from which to select primitives. A window is a rectangular region defined in world coordinates, and the range of data you wish to display must be within the window. Three cases must be considered. Primitives that are totally enclosed by the window can be transformed directly into display coordinates. Primitives that are completely outside the window can be ignored. Primitives that overlap the boundary of the window must be *clipped* to the window (see fig. 7.2). Each element of the object must be compared to each of the window's four edges, and the parts that are outside must be removed.

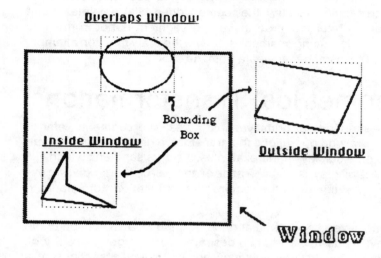

Fig. 7.2. Clipping primitives to the window.

Clipping Graphical Objects

The subject of clipping graphical objects to a rectangular region is widely understood, and several different techniques have been proposed. Following is a discussion of individual clipping routines that operate on points, rectangles, lines, and text, respectively.

Points

Clipping points to a window is easy to do; just apply some simple min-max operations to the point. This operation is coded as follows:

```
/* is point inside window? */
if( ( point.x <= window.right ) &&
    ( point.x >= window.left ) &&
    ( point.y <= window.top ) &&
    ( point.y >= window.bottom ))
    return( TRUE );
else
    return( FALSE );
```

Primitives with Bounding Boxes

Next, consider clipping primitives that are defined with a bounding box, such as rectangles and ovals. The bounding box is compared to the window to determine whether the primitive is to be completely or partially displayed. One utility routine defined earlier, the rectangle intersection function sect_rect(), provides the means to perform this operation. If an element's bounding box intersects the window, you must clip that element to the window and draw the clipped element on the display. The form of this operation is

```
/* define a result rectangle for the intersection */
rect_t  result;

/* bbox and window are pointers to rectangles */
if( sect_rect( bbox, window, &result ) == TRUE )
    {
    /* proceed to clip and draw primitive to display */
    ...
    }
```

If sect_rect returns TRUE, you need to perform detailed clipping of the element's parts. This state usually means that individual line segments must be examined for overlap.

Lines

Clipping lines to a window is more difficult than clipping points or rectangles. Use the Cohen-Sutherland algorithm, which is described in detail in the book *Fundamentals of Interactive Computer Graphics* by J. D. Foley and A. Van Dam.[1] The algorithm is straightforward and efficient. It begins by assigning four-bit *clip codes* to

---

[1] J. D. Foley and A. Van Dam, *Fundamentals of Interactive Computer Graphics* (1982; reprinted with corrections, Reading, M.A.: Addison-Wesley Publishing Company, 1983) pp. 144-149.

both endpoints of a line. The value of each bit indicates whether the endpoint is beyond one of the four boundaries of the window. By numbering the bits from left to right, you can assign the clip codes, as follows:

```
bit #1 = 1 => point is above the window
bit #2 = 1 => point is below the window
bit #3 = 1 => point is to the right of the window
bit #4 = 1 => point is to the left of the window
```

For example, a clip code of 1010 means that the endpoint is above (bit #1 set) and to the right (bit #3 set) of the clipping window. You can see all the possible combinations in the following diagram. (The clipping window is the center region.)

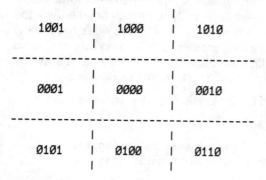

Note that a specific code exists for each of the nine possible regions. From these codes, you can determine when to *fracture* (separate into "in" and "out" parts) a line that crosses a window edge, or when to accept or reject an entire line. For example, if the clip codes for both line endpoints are zero (no bits are set), the line is trivially accepted. This operation is written as follows:

```
accept_check( code1, code2 )
int code1, code2;
{
    if( ! (code1 | code2) )
        return( TRUE );
    else
        return( FALSE );
}
```

Note that you use the bitwise OR symbol (|) rather than the symbol for logical OR (||). Because the codes have been defined to take advantage of these bitwise operations, the clipping algorithm is simple and fast. You also can check for trivial rejection by comparing the two clip codes to see whether they have any bits in common. This situation places both of a line's endpoints on the same side of the window exterior. The operation for trivial rejection is

```
reject_check( code1, code2 )
int code1, code2;
{
     if(code1 & code2)
          return( TRUE );
     else
          return( FALSE );
}
```

If the line cannot be accepted or rejected trivially, you must fracture the line by comparing it to each of the window's edges. Calculate the point where the window's edge and the line intersect, and then check again to make sure that you can accept the newly clipped line. In some cases, the line must be clipped to more than one window edge, but the algorithm takes this possibility into account. The format for the clipping function is

```
/* line clipping function */
BOOLEAN clipper(x1, y1, x2, y2, window_rect_pointer )

/* result of line clip, used as global variables */
int rx1, ry1, rx2, ry2;
```

The clipping function does not modify the input coordinates, but simply leaves the result of the clip in a set of predefined global variables. This feature provides for simple coding and fast execution. The function returns TRUE if the resulting line is accepted or clipped, and FALSE if the line is rejected (entirely outside the window).

Text

Finally, consider the clipping of text. You can take several approaches. One method is the "all or nothing" approach, in which complete characters are clipped. This method is fast and simple to implement. A more complicated method takes into account the strokes that form each character and clips them individually. This method usually is too complex to consider seriously in a highly interactive application. Another option is to let the display hardware do the clipping. When you draw text on the screen, call a system-dependent function with the text, the text's display position, and bounding box. The display hardware then can clip the text to the desired region. Although this method appears to be a very system-dependent operation, most graphics systems that support mixed text and graphics also support this type of text clipping.

The data that remains after the clipping operation must be mapped on the display. As noted, being able to define specific display areas in which to draw images is useful. These display areas are called viewports.

Using Viewports

Viewports are rectangular display regions (in display coordinates) in which graphical images are drawn. Several viewports can exist at any one time. Because this graphics system "assumes" that all viewports are unobscured, if viewports overlap on the display, the application must control which viewport is to be active. Do not overlap viewports on a display unless you intend to write additional code to manage them.

You create a viewport by calling the function new_vport(bitmap_rect_pointer). The function instantiates a viewport data structure, assigns the bit map rectangle coordinates to be those of the viewport, sets the background fill color to BLACK, and returns a pointer to the viewport data structure. The routine also draws a framed WHITE rectangle in the bit map and reduces the size of the viewport, so that all subsequent drawing to the viewport occurs within this frame. Each viewport is surrounded by a one-pixel border. The viewport C data structure is defined as

```
struct viewport
    {
    rect_t  *bitmap, /* bit map viewport */
            *window; /* segment window */
    int     brder,   /* border color, defaults to WHITE */
            bkgnd;   /* background color, defaults to BLACK */
    seg_t   *seg;
    };

    typedef struct viewport vport_t;
```

Special fields in this data structure support an application to manipulate segment data within a viewport without specifying both a segment and a window. With this feature, an application program can manipulate, through pans and zooms, the segment drawn within the viewport. To allow for this operation, assign a segment to the viewport through the function `set_vport_seg( view-port_pointer, segment_pointer )`. This operation sets the viewport structure's `window` field to be a copy of the bounding box of the seg-ment and makes the default a view of the entire segment.

To draw a segment in a viewport, use the function `draw_seg( seg-ment_pointer, viewport_pointer )`. If the segment has not been drawn previously in this viewport, `draw_seg` sets the clip window to be the segment's bounding box. This setting causes a default view of the entire segment. Note that `draw_seg` does not erase the view-port before the function draws the segment. Functions for manipu-lating segment images through a transformation-erase-draw sequence are described in the following paragraphs.

After a segment has been assigned to a viewport, you can ma-nipulate the way in which the segment is to be drawn. To pan (scroll) the segment in the viewport, use the function `pan_vport( viewport_pointer, dh, dv )`. This function offsets the viewport seg-ment window in the direction opposite from the dh (delta horizon-tal) and dv (delta vertical) arguments. This offset moves the segment within its window by values of dh and dv. For example, to move the image of a segment toward the upper right corner of a viewport, specify both dh and dv to be positive.

You can zoom in or out of a segment by using the function `zoom_vport( viewport_pointer, dh, dv )`. In this function, the dh and dv arguments specify values by which the viewport segment win-dow is reduced. To enlarge, or zoom in on, a viewport's segment, you must make the values of dh and dv positive. Conversely, to re-duce, or zoom out of, a viewport's segment, you must make these values negative. Note that by specifying different horizontal and vertical values to these functions, you can distort the displayed im-age of a segment.

To clear, or erase, a viewport, use the function `clear_vport( view-port_pointer )`. This function fills the viewport with a rectangle of the color `viewport_pointer->bkgnd`.

Mapping

The window represents the range of world coordinate data that you wish to display in a viewport. Given a window and a viewport, you must map each point within the window to a corresponding point within the viewport (see fig. 7.3). The mapping process is performed with the function map(x, y), which takes two integer pointers (to a world coordinate point), calculates the point's position within the viewport, and then resets the integers to be this pixel. The function for mapping world coordinates to a viewport is

```
map( x_pointer, y_pointer )
```

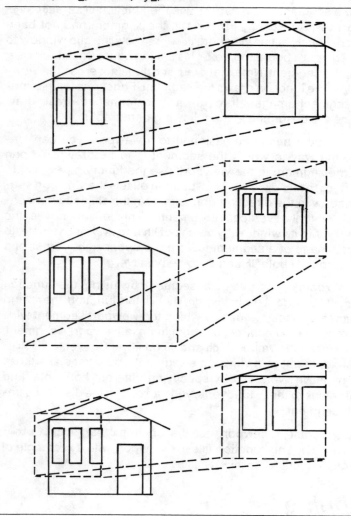

Fig. 7.3. Mapping segment data from clip window to viewport.

This use of pointers with the global result variables of the clipper provides a convenient method for mapping coordinates. To set up the mapping process, you must first tell the mapping function what the window and viewport rectangles are. This function, set_map, is

```
set_map( window_rect_pointer, viewport_rect_pointer )
```

This function is based on the assumption that the entire window is mapped to the bit map viewport. If the window and viewport have different aspect ratios (height to width ratios), graphical data is distorted by the mapping function. To avoid this mapping distortion, adjust the size of the world coordinate window so that its aspect ratio matches that of the viewport. This *remapping* of the windows is performed by the function

```
re_map( window_rect_pointer, viewport_rect_pointer )
```

The new window still contains all the original primitives. To set up a distortion-free mapping function for any viewport, call the following functions in the specified order:

```
/*
    viewport was predefined by the application
    cur_port is the current bit map viewport
    cur_win is the current window
*/
    cur_port = viewport->bitmap;
    cur_win = viewport->window;

    /* reset window aspect ratio to match viewport */
    re_map(cur_win, cur_port);

    /* set up mapping function from window to viewport */
    set_map(cur_win, cur_port);

    map( integer_pointer, integer_pointer );
    . . .
```

The map function is the performance bottleneck in the geometrical transformation process. This is because map uses double-precision floating-point operations to scale world coordinates to viewport (display) coordinates. To minimize the effects of this bottleneck, map only graphical elements that actually will be drawn on the display. That is, implement mapping only after all clipping has been performed. Mapping functions are discussed more fully in *Fundamentals of Interactive Computer Graphics*, pages 153-155.

Device Independence

To say that graphical software is completely device-independent is an exaggeration. A graphical system offers actual device independence only through its high-level commands and modeling operations. To implement the segmentation system on any specific piece of hardware, you must write some system-dependent code to act as a graphical-device driver.

The system-dependent code is organized in and should remain in a single file. The specific operations that you, the applications programmer, must write are few and easily coded. These functions are presented in table 7.1. When you want to transport the segmentation code to a new computer system, you need to rewrite only these functions. This feature gives a high degree of transportability to any application using this graphics system.

The Segmentation System Code

The code for the segmentation system has been divided into several small files. These files should be compiled separately into modules and linked to form the complete graphics system. The code modules can be compiled and linked on a system with as little as 128K of RAM. The complete listings, separated into several files, are given in the appendix A. The purpose and contents of each file are summarized in the following paragraphs.

The first file, defs.h, is a standard header that contains all the necessary structures, typedefs, and defines. This file must be #included in every application code module that uses the segmentation system.

The next two files create the primitives, segments, and keys. The file inst.c contains the fixed-length structure instantiation functions and some convenient append functions for segment construction. These functions are

Table 7.1.
Hardware Dependent Segmentation Functions

Function	Operations performed
initialize( )	Initialize bit map, Clear bit map (to BLACK) Set global screen rectangle
set_color(color)	Set new draw color to color
terminate( )	Terminate bit map
line(x, y)	Draw line from current position to current position plus x, y
line_to(x, y)	Draw line from current position to x, y in current color
text_bbox(string, jh, jv)	Return a rect pointer to the bounding box of the string (with justification)
draw_text(string, x, y, bbox)	Draw text string at x, y in the current draw color
fill_rect(rect_pointer)	Fill rectangle with current color
clear_vport(vport_pointer)	Fill viewport bit map with viewport background color
fill_oval(rect_pointer)	Fill oval with current color
frame_oval(rect_pointer)	Frame oval in current color
fill_poly(poly_pointer)	Fill polygon with current color

```
/*  instantiation functions */

key_t       *inst_key()
point_t     *inst_point(x, y)
rect_t      *inst_rect(left, bottom, right, top)
text_t      *inst_text(text, x, y, jh, jv)
ref_t       *inst_ref(name, x, y, seg)
seg_t       *inst_seg(name)

/* segment primitive append functions */
```

```
point(x, y)
rect(left, bottom, right, top)
oval(left, bottom, right, top)
text(text, x, y, jh, jv)
ref(name, x, y, seg)
```

The file cons.c contains the variable-length primitive construction functions. These functions provide dynamic allocation and construction of lines and polygons. The functions are:

```
begin_line()
line_t   *end_line()
begin_poly()
poly_t   *end_poly()
con_point(x, y)
```

The file utils.c contains the utility functions for point and rectangle calculations and the functions that calculate the bounding box of a segment. The file also includes an error-reporting function that is used throughout the segmentation system. The functions in utils.c are:

```
/* error-reporting function */

error(string)   /* string == *char */

/* utility functions */

pt_in_rect(r, pt)
loc_in_rect(r, x, y)
sect_rect(a, b, c)
union_rect(a, b, c)
rect_t *offset_rect(r, dh, dv)
rect_t *inset_rect(r, dh, dv)
rect_t *set_rect(r, left, bottom, right, top)
rect_t *copy_rect(or)

/* bounding box calculation functions */

rect_t *get_bbox(key)
rect_t *new_bbox()
set_bbox(bbox, x, y)
```

The file seg.c contains the functions that create, open, append, close, instance, delete, and draw segments. These functions maintain a linked list of segments in dynamic memory. The functions are

```
cr_seg(name)
op_seg(seg_pointer)
append(type, pointer)
seg_t    *cl_seg()
seg_t    *instance(seg_pointer)
del_seg(seg_pointer)
draw_seg(seg_pointer, vport_pointer)
```

The functions needed to read and write graphics metafiles are contained in file.c. If you do not need metafiles in your application, omit file.c. The metafile functions are:

```
/* read functions */

seg_t    *rd_seg(name)
key_t    *read_metafile(name)
key_t    *read_list(fp)
static   int    read_key(fp)

/* write functions */

wr_seg(seg)
write_metafile(name, key, bbox)
static   int    write_key(key, fp)
```

The next two files contain the functions for geometric operations. The file clip.c contains the line-clipping function that implements the Cohen-Sutherland clipping algorithm. The file map.c holds the functions for preparing and implementing the mapping of world coordinate data to display coordinate data. The functions for these two files are:

```
/* functions from clip.c */

clip_code(x, y, window)
reject_check(code1, code2)
accept_check(code1, code2)
clipper(x1, y1, x2, y2, window)

/* functions from map.c */
```

```
set_map(window, bit map)
re_map(window, bitmap)
map(x, y)
```

The next file, draw.c, contains functions for scanning linked lists of segment keys and decoding the attribute and primitive data for lower-level display-drawing routines. This file also includes functions for framing certain primitives. The functions are:

```
list_draw(key, viewport)
key_draw(key, viewport)
draw_line(l)
frame_rect(rect)
frame_poly(p)
```

The file view.c contains the functions for viewport creation and manipulation. These functions are:

```
vport_t *inst_vport()
vport_t *new_vport(bitmap)
set_vport_seg(vp, seg)
clear_vport(vp)
pan_vport(vp, dh, dv)
zoom_vport(vp, dh, dv)
```

The file graphics.c contains the system-dependent functions. *The code in this file should not be modified in any way.* To create a file for your system, make a copy of this file and edit the copy. To transport your application code, make a new copy of graphics.c and add the new system-dependent code to that copy. Using this procedure, you can accumulate system-dependent files under file names that match those systems. The file graphics.c also contains many print statements to help debug segmentation system code. The functions in this file are:

```
initialize()
set_color(attr)
terminate()
move_to(x, y)
move(x, y)
line_to(x, y)
line(x, y)
rect_t *text_bbox(string, jh, jv)
draw_text(string, jh, jv, x, y, bbox)
fill_rect(rect)
fill_oval(rect)
```

```
frame_oval(rect)
fill_poly(p)
```

The last file, diag.c, contains diagnostic functions. These functions provide a convenient way to debug the segmentation system code. The functions all begin with the characters prt_, and each function prints its information on the standard output device. The functions are:

```
prt_point( point_pointer )
prt_rect( rect_pointer )
prt_line( line_pointer )
prt_poly( poly_pointer )
prt_text( text_pointer )
prt_ref( ref_pointer )
prt_oval( rect_pointer )
prt_seg( segment_pointer )
```

The example about the house, presented earlier in this chapter, can now be specified in terms of the actual function calls. The complete code for this example follows. This code also provides an excellent testing of the segmentation system as it exercises a major portion of the functions.

```c
/* example program for segmentation system */

#include    "defs.h"
#define     NULL ØL


main()
{
/* declare function return types */
seg_t   *cl_seg(), *rd_seg();
vport_t *new_vport();

/* declare pointers to objects */
seg_t   *door, *window, *house, *city;

/* declare pointers to viewports */
vport_t *vp1, *vp2, *vp3;

    initialize();     /* graphics display */

/* create window segment */
```

```
    cr_seg("window");
        add_attr(RESET);
        rect(10, 10, 60, 80);
        rect(10, 00, 60, 90);
    window = cl_seg();

/* create door segment */

    cr_seg("door");
        add_attr(RESET);
        rect(10, 0, 100, 270);
    door = cl_seg();

/* create house segment */

    cr_seg("house");
        add_attr(RESET);
        rect(100, 100, 600, 500);
        begin_line();
        con_point(50, 480);
        con_point(350, 600);
        con_point(650, 480);
        add_line(end_line());
        ref("window", 150, 300, NULL);
        ref("window", 250, 300, NULL);
        ref("window", 350, 300, NULL);
        ref("door", 450, 100, NULL);
    house = cl_seg();

/* create city segment */

    cr_seg("city");
        ref("house", 0, 0, NULL);
        ref("house", 1000, 00, NULL);
        ref("house", 0, 700, NULL);
        ref("house", 1000, 700, NULL);
    city = cl_seg();

/* can write these segments to metafiles with */

    wr_seg(window);
    wr_seg(door);
    wr_seg(house);
    wr_seg(city);
```

```
/* then purge the segments from memory */

    del_seg(window);
   .del_seg(door);
    del_seg(house);
    del_seg(city);

/* later read the metafiles back into segments */

    window  = rd_seg("window");
    door    = rd_seg("door");
    house   = rd_seg("house");
    city    = rd_seg("city");

/* draw segments into three different viewports */

    /* Set up viewports */
    vp1 = new_vport(inst_rect(1, 1, 300, 500));
    vp2 = new_vport(inst_rect(1, 500, 600, 799));
    vp3 = new_vport(inst_rect(300, 1, 600, 500));

    /* assign segments to viewports */
    set_vport_seg(vp1, window);
    set_vport_seg(vp2, house);
    set_vport_seg(vp3, city);

    /* draw segments into viewports */
    draw_seg(window, vp1);
    draw_seg(house, vp2);
    draw_seg(city, vp3);

    sleep(10);
    terminate();      /* graphics display */
}
```

This chapter has presented all the techniques, data structures, and functions required to build a graphics application. The final two chapters present an in-depth study of how to apply these elements to build a modern interactive user interface.

8
Advanced User Interfaces: Concepts

The success or failure of an application often rests on how easily the application can be used. For instance, any application that requires a great deal of memorization is likely to scare away users, and the sight of a two-inch-thick user's manual is enough to discourage even an experienced programmer. This discouragement, however, can be prevented by a clear presentation of the application to users.

Creating an application that is user-friendly often requires more forethought and planning than creating the application itself. However, if a general-purpose user interface is developed and the functions are placed in a library, the amount of work required to implement a user-friendly application program is reduced greatly. In this chapter, the basic concepts of many popular user interfaces are discussed. Then, in the following chapter, the details and code for a user-friendly interface are given.

The User Interface

A *user interface* acts as a buffer between an application program and the user, allowing a user to customize the display of information according to personal preferences. User interfaces are inherently interactive and provide a continuing dynamic dialog between user and application. In this dialog, the user specifies actions called *events*. The application then interprets these events and responds appropriately. In other words, the interface is event driven, and actions on the user's part create or destroy displayed information.

Until recently, most user interfaces have consisted of little more than a command line interpreter. The system prompts the user for input by displaying a one-character symbol. The user responds by typing textual information, followed by a Return keystroke. Although this technique accomplishes the basic task of communication between user and machine, the method has many drawbacks. One such drawback is that the user must memorize or look up the command formats and effects.

Contemporary user interfaces often use graphical metaphors of real-world objects. For example, because file cabinets are used to store important documents, a user interface may use a picture of a file cabinet to represent a disk directory of document files. By extending such metaphors, you can create a system of recognizable objects. You manipulate these objects with another special object, the cursor. By directing the cursor, you select and control applications and their associated objects. User interfaces that use graphical displays, most of which are of the bit-mapped variety, are therefore the most flexible. With these interfaces, you can monitor the interaction with programs by watching the behavior of objects on the display. With the combination of a pointing device and conventional keyboard input, you can specify virtually any type of information.

The Cursor

The cursor (or pointer) can have many different shapes, ranging from simple arrows and crosses to more specialized symbols like human hands (see fig. 8.1). Usually the shape of the cursor is representative of the function being performed. For example, if the user is pulling, or *dragging*, a graphical image across the display, the cursor may appear as a hand. In cases where the system is processing some information and therefore temporarily ignoring user input, the cursor may take the shape of a watch or an hourglass. If the user is selecting an object on the screen, the cursor may default to a simple arrow. The cursor is the place where users focus their attention because the eye follows the selection process. When the shape of the cursor changes, the user is informed immediately of a pending operation.

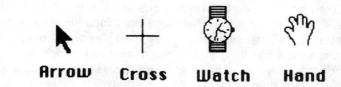

Fig. 8.1. Pointer shapes.

Arrow   Cross   Watch   Hand

Several methods of controlling the cursor's action are available. Perhaps the simplest technique is to use cursor-control keys. Pressing a cursor key causes the cursor to move a small distance in a given direction. Through successive keystrokes, you can move the cursor to any part of the display. The cursor keys are implemented easily, but are slow and cumbersome to use.

Pointing Devices

Pointing devices include the light pen and the touchscreen. The light pen, when placed next to a raster display, detects the exact time when the electron beam crosses the spot at which the pen is pointing. This time is measured against an internal clock, and the precise location of the pen is determined. With the touchscreen, you specify items with your finger. When you press your finger against the touchscreen, the computer determines your finger's location on the display. Both of these devices, however, require that you lift your hand to point at the display, which can be tiring during long sessions. In addition, the act of pointing covers the item you are selecting and limits the size of item that can be selected. Finally, light pens and touchscreens require specialized hardware, and this requirement restricts the number of systems on which these devices can be used.

Other devices used for pointing are the trackball and the joystick. The trackball, a small ball mounted on rollers, translates rotational movement into a change in the cursor's position. When the user rolls the ball in one direction, the cursor moves in the same direction. Because the ball can pick up significant momentum, the cursor can be made to move rapidly across the screen. The joystick is similar to the trackball. When you press the control stick in one direction, the cursor moves in that direction. Both the trackball and the joystick are useful for simple relative movements. In practice, however, information selection requires a more precise positioning device.

The most common positioning devices are the bit pad and the mouse. A bit pad consists of a hand-held locating device that moves on the surface of a specially designed platform. Movements of the locator are *absolute*. That is, each point on the platform corresponds to a location on the display screen. Bit pads usually are designed to give precise positioning, and therefore they can be expensive. The mouse, on the other hand, is simply an inverted hand-held trackball. Moving the mouse across any smooth surface (for example, a table top) causes an internal ball to roll, and this movement is translated into a corresponding movement of the cursor. Mouse movements are *relative*. That is, a movement of the mouse causes a corresponding change in the cursor position relative to the cursor's current position. If the mouse is picked up and placed on another part of the table, the movements continue from that new location. The mouse is relatively inexpensive and yet offers a fairly high-resolution capability. The mouse is often preferred over other pointing devices, because it gives comparatively high performance for the price.

Activation Buttons

Pointing devices also have *activation buttons*. The number of buttons varies according to the application's requirements, the type of positioning device, and the manufacturer. A single button is often best, because the user cannot press the wrong button! The more experienced user, however, may prefer the greater flexibility offered by several activation buttons. The process of pointing the device and pressing an activation button is called a *click*. Because the program can detect a series of rapid clicks, you can create activation functions. For example, in a text editing application, you can designate a single click for the selection of a new location for editing, a double click for the selection of a word, and a triple click for the selection of an entire line of text. These actions can be remembered easily by the user, and therefore productivity should increase.

The Desktop Metaphor

For the user to feel comfortable with an application, the interface must be consistent. That is, when the application changes modes, the method that the application uses to communicate with the user should remain the same. For example, if you are using the spreadsheet function of a business application and switch to a communication function, the user interface should have identical commands for operations common to both modes. Consistency of commands reduces the amount of memorization required for the user to operate the system and makes the program easier and more enjoyable to use.

An effective, natural-looking means of maintaining this consistency is the *desktop metaphor*. In this metaphor, the display shows an office desk and its tools (see fig. 8.2). The application functions being used also are displayed. Data elements called *icons* represent the functions and choices. An icon is a small graphical object that usually includes a label (see fig. 8.3). When you use the cursor to select an icon, the appearance of the icon changes to signify that the selection has occurred. You then can perform specific operations, such as move, copy, or open the icon. Moving and copying the icon are straightforward. Opening an icon causes the application that the icon represents to appear on the desktop. In addition, the icon itself may change in appearance or disappear. To delete an icon, you must activate the icon and drag it over another icon named trash. Just as you throw unwanted items into a garbage can, you can drag unwanted data, in the form of an icon, into the trash.

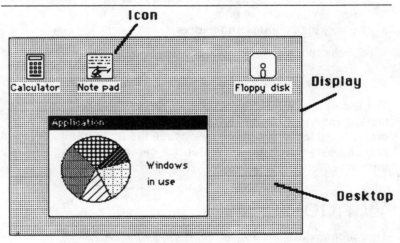

Fig. 8.2. The desktop.

Many different kinds of tools can be represented by icons. These tools can be divided into classes, much like the attribute classes given in Chapter 7. The following is a typical list of icon classes and their associated tools.

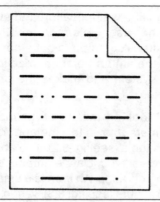

Fig. 8.3. A document icon.

desk accessories
    clock, calendar, calculator, note pad, etc.

file cabinets and folders (used to hold directories and files)
    applications
    application documents
    user documents
    help and manual documents
    other folders

supply cabinets (used to hold raw materials)
    new unused documents
    empty file cabinets and folders

miscellaneous
    trash
    floppy and hard disks

The use of icons is a clear, concise method of representing functions. Icons should be small enough that the desktop can hold several without looking cluttered. Because the appearance of icons can be customized, the user interface can gain greater flexibility and can be adopted readily.

Windows

This section presents the concept of the *window*. Note that the terminology used in this chapter is that which is commonly applied to graphical user interfaces. In Chapter 7, a window is a rectangle defined in world coordinates and used to select graphical data for display. In the following discussion, the word window means a graphical element used to display data on the desktop. The context of the discussion always should make clear which meaning of the term is being applied.

By extending the desktop metaphor, you can create many useful user interface structures, such as the metaphor of paper and ink. This metaphor is simple. You use paper and ink to create documents. The ink is ordinarily black, and the paper is white. You can use many different sheets of paper at one time, and these sheets can overlap. On the computer screen, the paper is a white rectangle on which data can be drawn in black. Many rectangles can exist at once and overlap on the display. To help you to keep track of the rectangles, a special area at the top of each rectangle shows a name (see fig. 8.4). In a similar fashion, other special regions can be defined. *Window* is the generic name given to such a graphical element.

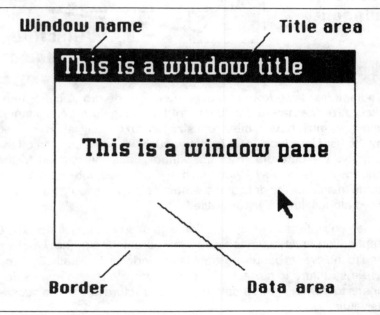

Fig. 8.4. A desktop window.

Through the use of windows, an application presents information in a user-controlled format. Only one window is *active* at any given time. The active window is the one with which you can interact. For example, you can modify the active window's size and location on the desktop. Windows are displayed in a depth-ordered fashion. The windows overlap, and by convention, the top window is the active one (see fig. 8.5). You can make any window active by placing the cursor in that window and clicking. If a window is obscured completely by other windows, you must sort through the pile of windows. As you would use ordinary sheets of paper, use windows to display information in a compact, easy-to-use format.

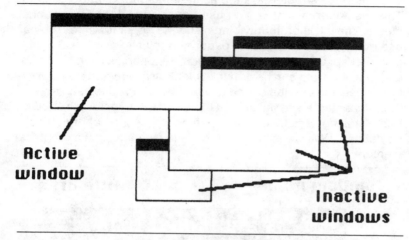

Fig. 8.5. Overlapping windows.

To implement windows in a user interface, the programmer must recognize the natural limitations of this metaphor. For instance, windows must have a minimum size, which usually is determined by the user interface itself. Also, because windows can run off the display, any data drawn to the window must be clipped to the bounds of the display. Windows can be deleted, too. However, in some instances the data that a window displays should not be deleted along with the window itself.

When you interface an application with one or more windows, the application must have access to the parameters of the windows and to the events occurring within the windows. Naturally, in C you use a structure to store a window's parameters. The application needs to maintain only a pointer to this structure in order to access its values.

To pass to an application the events occurring in a window, use pointers to functions. For many graphical regions of a window, save a pointer to a function that interprets the events for that region. For example, assume that a user clicks inside the data area of a window (see fig. 8.4). The user interface first determines the window in which the click takes place. If the click does not happen in any window, the event is passed to a desktop function that interprets the click. If the click occurs in an inactive window, that window is "popped" to the top of the window pile and made active. If the click occurs in the active window, the user interface checks the window's data structure to find a pointer to the function that processes the event. Provided that this function pointer is not NULL, the user interface calls the function with pointers to both the event and the window as parameters. According to the event's type, this function then determines what action is to be taken. The different function pointers that a window may use are shown in table 8.1.

Table 8.1
Function Pointers Used with Windows

Function Pointer	*Called*
keystroke	when key is pressed and cursor is in window
button	when click is made in window
close	when user deletes window
redraw	when user interface needs to refresh window

When you assign the same function pointers to different windows, the windows share functions. These function pointers give the user interface much of its power and flexibility.

Menus

You have learned the basic principles of user interfaces for applications and documents. However, you still need a way to command the interface. The standard method to control the user interface and its applications is through a *menu*. Menus contain logically related commands called *items*. Many different menus, each controlling a specific set of tasks, can exist in the user interface system. To invoke these tasks, select menu items with the cursor.

Menus are a special type of segment because the segment and its associated primitives can be animated graphically and the bounding boxes of each primitive are in display coordinates rather than world coordinates. This feature provides quick animation of graphical items without requiring the program to recalculate the display regions identified with the cursor. When the cursor enters the bounding box of a menu item, the item is highlighted (see fig.

8.6). When the cursor leaves the bounding box, the highlighting is dimmed; and the menu animation system tests the other items to find the cursor, which designates a new item to animate. To select an item, you simply click when the cursor is on that item. By using menus for command selection, you can point at both graphical items and commands in a consistent manner.

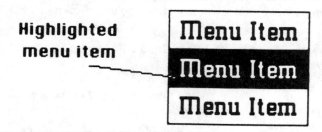

Fig. 8.6. Menu construction.

Many different methods of displaying and animating menus and their items are available. Usually, the type of menu an application uses depends on the application's purpose. If the application is an educational program, the commonly used menu items should be displayed at all times. Advanced users, however, often prefer to have menus displayed only when needed so that more display area is free for use.

Menus can be grouped into three basic categories: static, pop-up, and pull-down. *Static menus* are the easiest to implement. The items of a static menu are displayed on the computer screen at all times, as shown in figure 8.7. This type of menu is used for applications having few commands or programs designed for novice users. Because no command memorization is required, this arrangement pleases almost everyone. However, the value of static menus diminishes as the number of commands grows, because the menu itself occupies too much of the display area.

Pop-up menus get their name from the way they are activated. To activate a pop-up menu, place the cursor in a special graphical region (such as the interior or title bar of an active window) and click. The menu then "pops up" onto the screen under the cursor (see fig. 8.8). The function pointers in the window structure often direct events to trigger pop-up menus that request further action from the user. When a menu appears, the program is ready for you to select an item. When an item has been selected, the menu disappears. To allow the menu to be erased and the display area that the menu obscures to be restored, the function must save this area of the bit

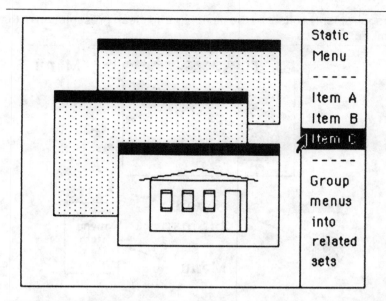

Fig. 8.7. A static menu.

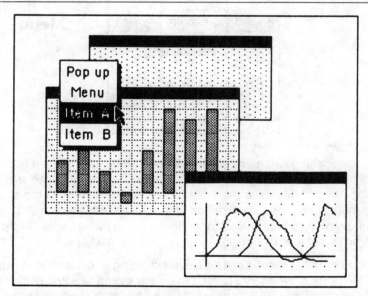

Fig. 8.8. A pop-up menu.

map in another part of memory before the menu is drawn. Then, when the item selection is completed, the previous bit map contents can be restored (see fig. 8.9). This type of menu requires you to remember which graphical regions invoke which menus. This requirement is offset by the flexibility and clean presentation of the menu.

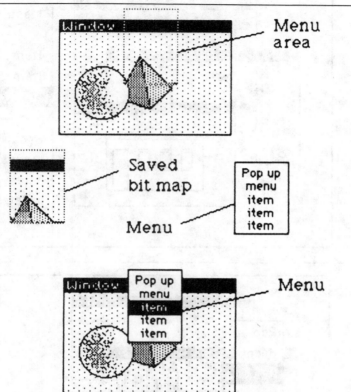

Fig. 8.9. Menu bit map elements.

The preceding two menu styles can be combined to form a hybrid called the *pull-down menu*. This menu incorporates the visual properties of the static menu and the efficient display of the pop-up menu. Each menu is given a name, which serves as a menu title. For example, a menu used for editing may be named edit. Typical items in this menu are undo, cut, copy, paste, and clear.

The titles of the menus are displayed in a single row across the top of the screen. When you place the cursor over a title and click, the corresponding menu pops up directly beneath the title (see fig. 8.10). You then "pull" the cursor down over the items to the desired item. If no item is selected before the cursor leaves the menu's area, the menu disappears and the bit map is restored. By combining static menu names with dynamic menu items, you achieve a hierarchical method of command selection.

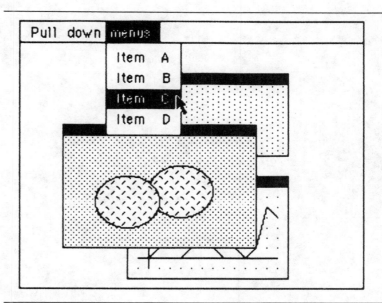

Fig. 8.10. A pull-down menu.

More than one type of menu can be used in one application program, and menu types can be combined. For example, a static menu can invoke pop-up menus. The static menu is the easiest to implement because no special bit map save and restore functions are needed. Pop-up and pull-down menus, however, offer greater flexibility. With the correct combinations of menus, a user interface can be a consistent and friendly tool.

This chapter has presented the rudimentary principles of interactive user interfaces. The basic ideas are simple. A cursor selects and manipulates graphical items for the purpose of program control. A constant and friendly dialog with the user is maintained through combinations of windows and menus. Finally, a common interface is used in which new applications can be developed and tested easily. The following chapter presents a set of C functions that implement many parts of the user interface and use the segmentation system.

9

Advanced User Interfaces: The System

This chapter gives the code for a user interface that implements the basic concepts explained in Chapter 8. The system described is not an application but a kernel of C functions from which application programs can be constructed. These functions should be compiled separately and linked in a user interface library. With this library, you can build powerful, easy-to-use programs quickly. The code for this library is in Appendix B. Screen images derived from the code in Appendix B are in Appendix C.

The user interface system is based on the segmentation system given in Chapter 7. The segmentation system, however, uses many viewports on the display. Those viewports describe nonoverlapping regions in which segments are to be drawn. The user interface system given in this chapter has a single permanent viewport that covers the entire display. The variable that points to this viewport is named the_port. Temporary viewports are used when the data segment from a window is to be drawn to a specific rectangular region.

This user interface displays as many windows as the system memory can hold. However, to be practical and to avoid crowding the desktop, you should specify a maximum number of windows. The simple type of window used consists of only title and data regions. Windows can share a data segment, and each window can represent a different view of that segment. The windows can be extended easily to provide more features.

Only the pop-up menu is provided in the basic system. Using the code from this menu, the applications programmer can create static and pull-down menus. Several default menus are installed. With these menus, the user controls the windows, their data segments, and the desktop. Any segment can be displayed in one or more windows.

Unlike the segmentation system, this user interface cannot be divided easily into device-independent and device-dependent files. Because the user interface is highly interactive, adding layers of code to the system to achieve device independence slows the dialog between application and user. Parts of the system can be considered independent of hardware yet dependent on the segmentation system.

Basic Configuration

The user interface system is designed from the top down (see Chapter 1). At the highest level, the user interface is a group of *functionality managers*. Each functionality manager is a collection of functions controlling different aspects of the interaction between user and application. These functions are the display, the event, the menu, and the window managers (fig. 9.1). The general properties of each subsystem are presented first. Then each subsystem is examined in more detail.

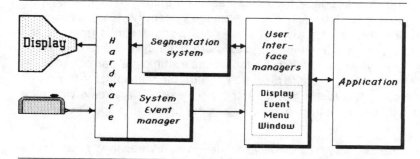

Fig. 9.1. Basic configuration of user interface system.

The Functionality Managers

The *display manager* performs operations specific to the display of the desktop and to the cursor, such as controlling the cursor's shape and display status. An application can change the cursor's position, request the cursor's current position, or hide or display the cursor. For instance, during any bit-map write operation, the cursor must be hidden to prevent conflict in the bit map between the cursor and the information displayed. The user interface automatically hides the cursor during the write operation.

The display manager also creates the segment for the desktop. This segment must fill the display and may include icons and static menus. Because the desktop segment refreshes the display, this segment never should be deleted. Several default desktop menu operations are provided. These include quitting the program, closing all displayed windows, and printing the image of the display. To activate the menu that invokes these functions, you click on any unoccupied region of the desktop.

The *event manager* is the section of code in which user-specified actions are interpreted and passed to the rest of the system. With this manager, hardware-specific events—such as cursor movement, button actions, and keystrokes—are detected. Keystrokes are filtered through a simple lookup table, which redefines the keys and makes the use of special keys easy. Once an event is detected, the event manager fills an event data structure with the event's type, cursor position, and keystrokes, as applicable. Then a pointer to this event structure is returned to the event manager's calling function.

The *menu manager* contains the functions that provide menu creation, animation, and bit-map save and restore operations. Pop-up menus are invoked by calling a menu function with arguments consisting of the number of menu items and a pointer to an array of character pointers. When an item is selected, this function returns the array index of the item; otherwise, the value negative one (-1) is returned. Through successive calls to this function, an application prompts the user for command information.

Of all the managers, the *window manager* is the most complex. This manager controls the creation, display, modification, and deletion of windows on the desktop. The window manager also refreshes specific rectangular regions of the display, including all windows and desktop items. The manager provides a set of default window operations for new windows. For example, a window modification menu can be invoked by clicking in the title area of the active window. From this menu, the user can move, size, or close the active window (see fig. 9.2). When a window is moved or sized, a rectangle matching the window's outline appears on the display (see figs. 9.3a and 9.3b). The user moves or reshapes the rectangle and then clicks the activation button, and the window is redrawn in the new area. When a window is closed, the region of the display that was obscured by that window automatically is refreshed.

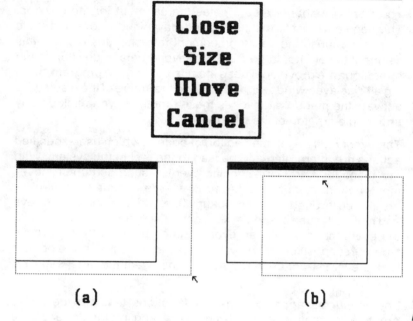

Fig. 9.2. Window modification menu.

(a)

(b)

Fig. 9.3a. Moving a window.

Fig. 9.3b. Sizing a window.

The window manager also provides several default window data manipulation operations that are activated by selecting a menu item. These manipulation operations are: fit (data to window), en-large (zoom in), reduce (zoom out), and scroll (data in window). The fit operation simply sets the window to the segment's bounding box, the clipping rectangle for the data segment, so that the entire data segment is visible. The scroll operation pops up a menu that requests the direction in which the data segment is to be scrolled. The choices are up, down, left, and right (fig. 9.4). A special function detects the window in which an event has occurred. Inactive windows can be identified and made active through a user's click. The window manager contains all the window-specific functions, which are independent of hardware but dependent on the segmentation system.

Fig. 9.4. Window view menus.

The Event Loop

As explained in the previous chapter, a user interface is event driven. Events, specified by the user and interpreted by the event manager, are processed in what is called an *event loop*. An event loop is a while loop in which specific events are examined until some condition is satisfied. For example, the menu animation function animates menu items until you issue a button event to select an item. Clearly, you need a master event loop in which general user actions are examined. This event loop is placed in the main routine and is sketched as follows:

```
/* enter main event loop ... */
while( event->type != ABORT_EVENT )
{
event = get_next_event();

switch( event->type )
    {
    case  NULL_EVENT    :
        break;

    case  KEY_EVENT    :
        /* find out where keystroke event happened */
        my_window = what_window( event->where )

        /* Was it on the desktop? */
        if( my_window == NULL)
            desktop( event );
```

```
                    /* Was it in the active window? */
                    else if( my_window == front_window())
                        {
                        /* perform window keystroke actions */
                        }

                    /* must have happened in an inactive window */
                    else
                        {
                        pop_window( my_window );
                        /* perform window keystroke actions */
                        }

                break;

            case  BUTTON_EVENT  :
                    /* find out where button event happened */
                    my_window = what_window( event->where )

                    /* Was it on the desktop? */
                    if( my_window == NULL)
                        desktop( event );

                    /* Was it in the active window? */
                    else if( my_window == front_window())
                        {
                        /* perform window button actions */
                        }

                    /* must have happened in an inactive window */
                    else
                        {
                        pop_window( my_window );
                        /* perform window button actions */
                        }

                break;
            }
        }
```

Note carefully the structure of the preceding code fragment. The
while loop continues until a specific event occurs, namely the
event that directs the program to abort. During the processing of

other events, the code may call other functions, each of which can have other event loops.

The header file, named usrif.h, contains all user interface structures and macro definitions, including event and window structures, function return types, and maximum numbers for pop-up menu items and displayed windows. This file also contains an include statement for the segmentation system header file defs.h. The header file usrif.h must be included in every application file that uses the user interface.

The Display Manager

The display manager functions are contained in the file display.c. These functions control the cursor's appearance and manage events that occur on the desktop.

The cursor function set_cursor(point_pointer) sets the cursor's position (in display coordinates). This function is passed a pointer to a point structure. To request the cursor's current position, you call a similar function named get_cursor(point_pointer). To hide the cursor (remove it from the display), you call the function hide_cursor(). To redisplay the cursor, you call the function show_cursor(). The hide_cursor() function increments and the show_cursor() decrements a variable that determines whether the cursor is displayed.

The desktop segment is created by the function make_desktop(). This function instantiates a new segment containing the graphical primitives that make up the desktop image and sets the global segment pointer variable desk_seg to the desktop segment.

All events that occur on the desktop are processed by the display manager function desktop(event_pointer). This function takes an event structure pointer as the function argument and pops up the menu for modification of the desktop.

The Event Manager

The functions of the event manager provide the low-level interface between user and computer. These functions are contained in the file event.c. Normally, event-processing functions are system dependent. The functions provided here isolate the system-dependent routines from the rest of the user interface so that the events are processed uniformly throughout the user interface regardless of environment.

To describe an event to both the user interface and the applications that reside within the user interface, you define a C data structure that holds all the information associated with the event. This structure contains three fields: what the event was, where the cursor was during the event, and what keystroke data, if any, was entered. This structure is defined as

```
struct   event_record
{
int      what;
char     stroke;
point_t where;
};

typedef struct event_record event_t;
```

Following standard C programming style, the what field is set to one of several predefined constants. These constants, which are known throughout the user interface from the usrif.h header file, are:

```
/* event manager type definitions */
#define NULL_EVENT          0
#define DN_BUTTON_EVENT     1
#define UP_BUTTON_EVENT     2
#define KEY_EVENT           3
#define ABORT_EVENT         4
```

These definitions describe an event's type. NULL_EVENT means that no activation event has occurred. (However, the cursor position may have changed.) The next two events describe the pressing of an activation button. If more than one activation button is available, the stroke field contains another constant, which indicates that a button has been pressed. KEY_EVENT shows that a keystroke has been made. Again, the stroke field contains the character of the key that was pressed; the character value is taken from the lookup table. ABORT_EVENT signals the application or the user interface to stop processing and return to the main event loop. This event type serves to an interrupt time-consuming processes.

The event manager must be initialized at system start-up. The function that performs this operation is init_event(). The variables set during this initialization phase are the cursor position and the values contained in the keyboard lookup table. Any needed system-dependent routines also are called from this function.

To ask the event manager for the next user-specified event, you call the function get_next_event(). This function returns a pointer to the structure that contains the event parameters. The function "assumes" that the system is queuing events to the event manager, which never misses a queued event. If your operating system does not queue events, you can define your own queue, as explained in Chapter 5.

The Menu Manager

The menu manager consists of four functions that provide pop-up menu facilities. These functions are contained in the file menu.c. To create a pop-up menu, you first must define an array of character pointers that describe the individual menu items. For example, the edit menu of Chapter 8 can be defined with the following array:

```
char    *edit_menu[6] =
    {
    "Cancel",
    "Undo",
    "Cut",
    "Copy",
    "Paste",
    "Clear"
    };
```

To animate this menu, call the function pop_up_menu(6, edit_menu). The function creates a menu with the specified items, animates the menu until the user makes a selection, and returns an index to the selected item. For this example, the constants for the menu items are defined as

```
/* edit menu item constants */
#define CANCEL  0
#define UNDO    1
#define CUT     2
#define COPY    3
#define PASTE   4
#define CLEAR   5
```

If you select PASTE, for instance, the function returns an integer value of 4. Defining macro names for each menu item's index is convenient and improves the readability of the code.

The menu.c file also contains the segment animation function for selecting menu items and the bit-map save and restore functions. As stated earlier, the basic pop-up menu code in this file can be extended easily to provide pull-down and static menu.

The Window Manager

The window manager controls the desktop's set of windows. The functions for this manager are contained in the file window.c. A special structure has been defined to hold a window's associated parameters:

```
struct  window_record
    {
    int (*key_fn)(),          /* window key function */
        (*button_fn)();       /* window button function */
    char    *name;
    seg_t   *shape, *data;
    rect_t  *data_win,
            *area,
            *title,
            *pane;
    struct  window_record *next, *prev;
    };

    typedef struct window_record window_t;
```

The first two fields of this structure are pointers to functions that interpret events occurring within the window's data display region. The first one, key_fn, is for keystroke events, and the second, button_fn, handles activation button events. Several other functions, such as window-close and window-data-draw functions, can be added. For example, a new draw function could be used to draw data in a different coordinate system. The next field in the window structure is a character pointer to the name of the window. The shape and data fields contain pointers to the segments that describe, respectively, the shape of the window and the data to be displayed within the window. The next four rectangle pointers contain the window's data_win, or clipping, region (in world coordinates); the area that the window occupies on the desktop; the area that the title occupies; and the bit map (pane) in which the window's data segment is to be drawn. When a window is sized or moved on the desktop, the area, title, and pane rectangles and the shape segment must be adjusted. The last two pointer variables describe the doubly linked list structure that contains the window structures. This list of window structures is depth ordered; the top, or active, window always is kept at the beginning of the list. The manager uses two static window pointer variables, front and back, to maintain the list. This window structure can be extended to meet the needs of any application.

The window manager, like the event manager, must be initialized at start-up by the function init_window(). This function instantiates the permanent viewport that the user interface uses and initializes a viewport pointer called the_port. The function also calls another function, make_desktop(), to create the desktop segment and prepares a static rectangle, which determines a new window's position on the display.

To create a new window, you call the function new_window(name, segment_pointer, rectangle_pointer). This function takes as its arguments a character pointer to the window's name, a segment pointer to the data segment to be drawn in the window, and a pointer to a rectangle describing the window's position on the desktop. The new_window function draws the window, makes it active, and returns a window pointer to the new window structure. The default view of a data segment, when passed to new_window, is of the entire segment. That is, the bounding box of the segment describes the segment's clipping region. If no particular window size is required, you can insert into the argument for the window's rectangular area a call to the function new_rect(). Each time new_rect is called, the function returns a pointer to a rectangle that is offset from the last time the function was called. This way, windows do not obscure each other on the desktop.

To pop a window (bring to the beginning of the list and make the window active), you call the function

```
pop_window( window_pointer )
```

This function resets the list pointers and redraws the window to make it the active one.

Several functions are useful for detecting events within a window. The first, front_window(), returns a pointer to the active window. The next function, what_window(point_pointer), returns a pointer to the front-most window in which a point lies. If the point is not in any window, the function returns NULL. With this function, you can determine in which window, if any, an event has occurred. The remaining detection functions determine whether a point is in a window and, if so, in what part of a window the point lies. These functions are in_window(point_pointer, window_pointer), in_title(point_pointer, window_pointer), and in_pane(point_pointer, window_pointer). These BOOLEAN functions return TRUE or FALSE and determine what type of action is required in response to an event.

The next two functions are called when an event occurs within a window's displayed area. The first function, mod_window(event_pointer, window_pointer), is called when you click in the title area of a window. This function pops up a menu from which you can size, move, or close the window. The second function is called through the button_fn field in the window's structure. The new_window function sets this field to a function that pops up a menu for modifying the view of the window's data segment. This function is called view_window(event_pointer, window_pointer). Note that both functions take as their arguments an event and a window pointer. Any application-defined function that takes the place of these functions also must take these two arguments. From these arguments, a window function can perform the necessary response to events.

The next window manager functions control the drawing and redrawing of the desktop and its windows. The first function, which draws a window on the display, is draw_win(window_pointer). The next, draw_all(), refreshes the entire display. The latter function first draws the desktop and then draws each window, successively from back to front. This progression gives the display its depth-ordered appearance.

Often, while moving or sizing a window, you need to refresh only a specific rectangular region. This operation requires careful tracking of the parts of the windows to be redrawn. To draw a single window in a given rectangle, you call the function win_inrect(window_pointer, rectangle_pointer). This function remaps the viewport and data segment clip region to provide the correct transformation of the shape and data segments (see figs. 9.5a, 9.5b, and 9.5c). To refresh the display within a given rectangle, you call the function all_wins(rectangle_pointer). This function performs in the specified rectangle the same operations as draw_all() does for the entire display.

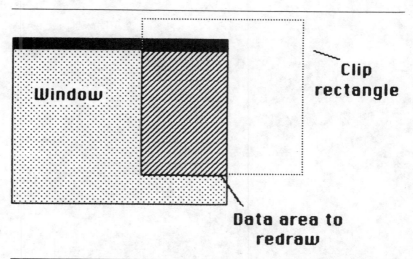

Fig. 9.5. Clipping a window to a rectangle.

The last two window manager functions control the removal of windows from the desktop. Note that these functions *do not* delete a window's data structure or any of its associated parameters. Instead, the user interface "assumes" that the application itself controls these deletion operations. The first function is `purge_window( window_pointer )`. This function removes a window data structure from the doubly linked list of windows. The second function, `purge_all()`, removes all windows from the depth list. These functions are called from the window modification function and the desktop menu function, respectively.

Overview

This text has explained how to implement the basic functions performed by an advanced user interface. The desktop, menu, and window functions support a consistent, graphical dialog between user and application. The C code provided here is best used as a kernel for developing user-friendly applications. The creative use of this code with a developer's own enhancements can produce professional, easy-to-use software systems.

Appendix A
The Segmentation
System Code

The following files comprise the source code for the segmentation system presented in Chapter 7, "Application Graphics." This code consists of a single header file and 11 code files. To create the segmentation system, standard C program compilation techniques should be used. Each source code file is compiled to a linkable object file. All object files are then linked together to form the segmentation system file, segsys. o. This object file is then linked with an application file to create the binary program file. The following makefile may be used on UNIX™ systems to create the segmentation system.

```
#Make file for segmentation system
OBJECTS = clip.o cons.o diag.o file.o graphics.o\
          inst.o map.o seg.o utils.o view.o

#executable binary file is called 'program,' application code 'main.c'

program: defs.h main.c segsys.o
     cc -o program main.c segsys.o

segsys.o: defs.h OBJECTS
     cc -o segsys.o OBJECTS

clip.o:    defs.h clip.c
     cc -c clip.c

cons.o:    defs.h cons.c
     cc -c clip.c
```

```
diag.c:    defs.h diag.c
     cc -c diag.c

draw.c:    defs.h draw.c
     cc -c draw.c

file.o:    defs.h file.c
     cc -c file.cx

graphics.o:    defs.h graphics.c
     cc -c graphics.c

inst.o:    defs.h inst.c
     cc -c inst.c

map.o:    defs.h map.c
     cc -c map.c

seg.o:    defs.h seg.c
     cc -c seg.c

utils.o:    defs.h utils.c
     cc -c utils.c

view.o:    defs.h view.c
     cc -c view.c

#end of make file for segmentation system
```

main.c

```
/*
    main.c

    test program for segmentation system
*/

#include        "defs.h"
#define    NULL ØL


void    main()
{
/* function returns to be moved to globals.h */
seg_t   *cl_seg(), *rd_seg();
vport_t *new_vport();
```

```
/* pointers to items */
seg_t   *door, *window, *house, *city;

/* pointers to viewports */
vport_t *vp1, *vp2, *vp3;

int     i, j, k;

    initialize();      /* graphics display */

/* create-window segment */

        cr_seg("window");
        add_attr(RESET);
        rect(10, 10, 60, 80);
        rect(10, 00, 60, 90);
        window = cl_seg();

/* create-door segment */

        cr_seg("door");
        add_attr(RESET);
        rect(10, 0, 100, 270);
        door = cl_seg();

/* create-house segment */

        cr_seg("house");

        add_attr(RESET);
        rect(100, 100, 600, 500);
        begin_line();
        con_point(50, 480);
        con_point(350, 600);
        con_point(650, 480);
        add_line(end_line());

        ref("window", 150, 300, NULL);
        ref("window", 250, 300, NULL);
        ref("window", 350, 300, NULL);

        text("House",  0,  0, LEFT , BOTTOM);
```

```
            ref("door", 450, 100, NULL);

      house = cl_seg();

/* create-city segment */

          cr_seg("city");

          add_attr(RESET);
          ref("house", 0, 0, NULL);
          ref("house", 1000, 00, NULL);
          ref("house", 0, 700, NULL);
          ref("house", 1100, 800, NULL);

          text("City Block", 0, -100, LEFT , BOTTOM);


          city = cl_seg();

/* can write these segments to metafiles with */

      wr_seg(window);
      wr_seg(door);
      wr_seg(house);
      wr_seg(city);

/* purge segments from memory */

      del_seg(window);
      del_seg(door);
      del_seg(house);
      del_seg(city);

/* later read metafiles back into segments */

      window  = rd_seg("window");
      door    = rd_seg("door");
      house   = rd_seg("house");
      city    = rd_seg("city");

/* draw segments in three different viewports */
```

```
    /* set up viewports */
    vp1 = new_vport(inst_rect(1, 1, 300, 500));
    vp2 = new_vport(inst_rect(1, 500, 600, 799));
    vp3 = new_vport(inst_rect(300, 1, 600, 500));

    /* assign segments to viewports */
    set_vport_seg(vp1, window);
    set_vport_seg(vp2, house);
    set_vport_seg(vp3, city);

    /* draw segments in viewports */
    draw_seg(window, vp1);
    draw_seg(house, vp2);
    draw_seg(city, vp3);

    for(j=0; j<100; j++)
        {
        pan_vport(vp2, 5, 5);
        zoom_vport(vp3, -10, -10);
        }

    sleep(10);
    terminate();     /* graphics display */
}
```

defs.h

```
/*
    defs.h

    segment, key, primitive, and attribute declarations
*/

#define NULL 0L

#define BOOLEAN int
#define TRUE 1
#define FALSE  0

#define BIG  (60*1024)
#define NBIG (-BIG)

char    *malloc(), *calloc();
#define MALLOC(x)   ((x *) malloc(sizeof(x)))
#define CALLOC(n, x) ((x *) calloc(n, sizeof(x)))
```

```
struct  point_primitive
    {
    int x, y;
    };

typedef struct  point_primitive point_t;
point_t *inst_point();

struct  rect_primitive
    {
    int left, bottom, right, top;
    };

typedef struct  rect_primitive  rect_t;
rect_t  *inst_rect();

struct  cont_point
    {
    point_t point;
    struct  cont_point  *next;
    };

typedef struct  cont_point  cpoint_t;

struct  line_primitive
    {
    int     num_points;
    rect_t *bbox;
    struct  cont_point  *point;
    };

typedef struct  line_primitive  line_t;
line_t  *inst_line();
line_t  *close_line();

struct  poly_primitive
    {
    int     num_points;
    rect_t  *bbox;
    struct  cont_point  *point;
    };
```

```
typedef struct  poly_primitive  poly_t;
poly_t  *inst_poly();
poly_t  *close_poly();

#define oval_t  rect_t
#define inst_oval    inst_rect

/*
    text justification definitions
*/

#define TOP      't'
#define CENTER   'c'
#define BOTTOM   'b'
#define LEFT     'l'
#define MIDDLE   'm'
#define RIGHT    'r'
#define TXTSZE   32

struct  text_primitive
    {
    point_t origin;
    rect_t  *bbox;
    char    just[2];    /* justification */
    char    text[TXTSZE];
    };

typedef struct  text_primitive  text_t;
text_t  *inst_text();

struct  reference
    {
    point_t origin;
    struct  segment *instance;
    char    name[TXTSZE];
    };

typedef struct  reference   ref_t;
ref_t   *inst_ref();

/*
    key primitive types
*/
```

```
#define POINT    1
#define LINE     2
#define RECT     3
#define POLY     4
#define OVAL     5
#define TEXT     6
#define REF      7
#define ISPRIM(x)    ((x) < 8 ? TRUE : FALSE)

struct  seg_key
    {
    int type;
    union
        {
        char    *ptr;
        point_t *point;
        line_t  *line;
        rect_t  *rect;
        poly_t  *poly;
        oval_t  *oval;
        text_t  *text;
        ref_t   *ref;
        }   key;
    struct  seg_key *next;
    };

typedef struct  seg_key key_t;
key_t   *inst_key();

/*
    dynamic segment construction macros
*/

#define add_attr(a)     append(a, NULL)
#define add_point(p)    append(POINT, p)
#define add_line(l)     append(LINE, l)
#define add_rect(r)     append(RECT, r)
#define add_poly(p)     append(POLY, p)
#define add_oval(o)     append(OVAL, o)
#define add_text(t)     append(TEXT, t)
#define add_ref(r)      append(REF, r)
```

```
/*
    attribute definitions
*/

#dexfine RESET    99

#define COPY      10
#define XOR       11

#define FILL      12
#define NOFILL    13
#define FRAME     14
#define NOFRAME   15

#define BLACK     20
#define RED       21
#define GREEN     22
#define BLUE      23
#define CYAN      24
#define MAGENTA   25
#define YELLOW    26
#define WHITE     27

#define ISATTR(x)   ((x) >= 10 ? TRUE : FALSE)

/*
    segment descriptor
*/

struct  segment
    {
    int num_inst, visible, locked;
    char    *name;
    rect_t *bbox;
    key_t  *data,
            *eol;
    struct  segment *next;
    };

typedef struct  segment seg_t;
seg_t   *cl_seg();  /* close segment */
```

```
/*
    viewport descriptor
*/

struct  viewport
    {
    rect_t  *bitmap,
            *window;
    int     brder, bkgnd;   /* colors */
    seg_t   *seg;
    };
typedef struct  viewport    vport_t;

/*
    metafile key
*/

struct    diskkey
    {
    int type;
    int size;
    };
typedef    struct    diskkey    disk_key_t;
```

clip.c

```
/*
    clip.c

    line-clipping routines using
    Cohen-Sutherland clipping algorithm
*/

#include "defs.h"

#define BIT1    1
#define BIT2    2
#define BIT3    4
#define BIT4    8

/* result of line clip */
int rx1, ry1, rx2, ry2;
```

```
/*
    clip codes for line endpoints


        |         |
    1001    |  1000   |  1010
        |         |

-------------------------------------
        |         |
    0001    |  0000   |  0010
        |         |

-------------------------------------
        |         |
    0101    |  0100   |  0110
        |         |
*/

int clip_code(x, y, window)
int     x, y;
rect_t  *window;
{
int code = 0;

    if(x < window->left)
        code += BIT1;
    else if(x > window->right)
        code += BIT2;

    if(y < window->bottom)
        code += BIT3;
    else if(y > window->top)
        code += BIT4;

    return(code);
}

/*  trivial rejection check */

BOOLEAN reject_check(code1, code2)
int code1, code2;
{
    if(code1 & code2)
        return(TRUE);
```

```
    else
        return(FALSE);
}

/* trivial acceptance check */

BOOLEAN accept_check(code1, code2)
int code1, code2;
{
    if( ! (code1 | code2) )
        return(TRUE);
    else
        return(FALSE);
}

/* clip routine */

BOOLEAN clipper(x1, y1, x2, y2, window)
int x1, y1, x2, y2;
rect_t  *window;
{
int     code1, code2 ,done, accept, temp, swaps;
double  n, d;

    swaps = 0;
    done = accept = FALSE;

    while(done == FALSE)
        {
        code1 = clip_code(x1, y1, window);
        code2 = clip_code(x2, y2, window);

        if(reject_check(code1, code2))
            done = TRUE;
        else
            {
            accept = accept_check(code1, code2);
            if(accept)
                done = TRUE;
            else
                /* subdivide line because one
                    point at most is inside window */
```

```
{
if(code1 == 0)
    {   /* make point 1 outside */
    swaps++;
    temp = x1;      x1 = x2;        x2 = temp;
    temp = y1;      y1 = y2;        y2 = temp;
    temp = code1;   code1 = code2;  code2 = temp;
    }

if(code1 & BIT4)    /* divide at top of window */
    {
    n = (double) ((x2 - x1) * (window->top - y1));
    d = (double) (y2 - y1);

    x1 = x1 + (int) (n / d);
    y1 = window->top;
    }
else if(code1 & BIT3)   /* divide at bottom of window */
    {
    n = (double) ((x2 - x1) * (window->bottom - y1));
    d = (double) (y2 - y1);

    x1 = x1 + (int) (n / d);
    y1 = window->bottom;
    }

else if(code1 & BIT2)    /* divide at right of window */
    {
    n = (double) ((y2 - y1) * (window->right - x1));
    d = (double) (x2 - x1);

    y1 = y1 + (int) (n / d);
    x1 = window->right;
    }
else if(code1 & BIT1)   /* divide at left of window */
    {
    n = (double) ((y2 - y1) * (window->left - x1));
    d = (double) (x2 - x1);.
```

```
                        y1 = y1 + (int) (n / d);
                        x1 = window->left;
                        }
                    }
                }   /* end of no reject */
            }   /* end of while */

        if(accept)
            {
            if(swaps & 1) /* swap points back to original order */
                {
                rx1 = x2;   rx2 = x1;
                ry1 = y2;   ry2 = y1;
                }
            else
                {
                rx1 = x1;   rx2 = x2;
                ry1 = y1;   ry2 = y2;
                }
            return(TRUE);
            }
        else
            return(FALSE);
}
```

cons.c

```
/*
    cons. c

    Complex primitive construction routines
*/

#include    "defs. h"

static  line_t      *l      =   NULL;
static  poly_t      *p      =   NULL;
static  cpoint_t    *cur    =   NULL;
static  cpoint_t    *first  =   NULL;
static  rect_t  *bbox = NULL;
rect_t  *new_bbox();
```

```
void      con_point(x, y)
int       x, y;
{
cpoint_t    *cp;

    if( (cp = CALLOC(1, cpoint_t)) == NULL)
        error("Can't instantiate Continue Point");
    else
        {
        if(first == NULL)
            first = cur = cp;
        else
            {
            cur->next = cp;
            cur = cur->next;
            }

        cur->point.x = x;
        cur->point.y = y;
        set_bbox(bbox, x, y);
        }
}


void      begin_line()
{
    if((l != NULL) | (p != NULL))
        {
        error("Can't reopen line, close current primitive");
        return;
        }

    if( (l = CALLOC(1, line_t)) == NULL)
        error("Can't instantiate line");

    bbox = new_bbox();
}

line_t      *end_line()
{
line_t      *temp;
cpoint_t  *cp;
int     i = 0;
```

```
        if(first == NULL)
            error("Line contains zero points");

        if(l == NULL)
            {
            error("Can't close unopened line");
            return(NULL);
            }
        else
            {
            l->point = first;
            cp = first;
            while(cp != NULL)
                {
                i++;
                cp = cp->next;
                }

            l->num_points = i;
            l->bbox = bbox;
            bbox = NULL;

            temp = l;

            /* reset for the next line */
            first = cur = l = NULL;
            return(temp);
            }
}

void    begin_poly()
{
    if((l != NULL) | (p != NULL))
        {
        error("Can't reopen polygon, close current primitive");
        return;
        }

    if( (p = CALLOC(1, poly_t)) == NULL)
        error("Can't instantiate polygon");

    bbox = new_bbox();
}
```

```
poly_t    *end_poly()
{
poly_t    *temp;
cpoint_t  *cp;
int    i = 0;

    if(first == NULL)
        error("Poly contains zero points");
    if(p == NULL)
        {
        error("Can't close unopened poly");
        return(NULL);
        }
    else
        {
        /* make sure that last point == first point ! */
        if((first->point.x != cur->point.x) ||
           (first->point.y != cur->point.y))
            con_point(first->point.x, first->point.y);

        p->point = first;
        cp = first;
        while(cp != NULL)
            {
            i++;
            cp = cp->next;
            }

        p->num_points = i;
        p->bbox = bbox;
        bbox = NULL;

        temp = p;
        first = cur = p = NULL;
        return(temp);
        }
}
```

diag.c

```
/*
    diag.c

    diagnostic routines
*/
```

```c
#include "defs.h"

char  mess[] = "DIAG : Attribute : ";

void    prt_point(p)
point_t    *p;
{
    printf("DIAG : Point %d, %d\n", p->x, p->y);
}

void    prt_rect(r)
rect_t *r;
{
    printf("DIAG : Rect left/bottom %d, %d right/top %d, %d\n",
        r->left, r->bottom, r->right, r->top);
}

void    prt_line(l)
line_t *l;
{
cpoint_t    *cp;

    printf("DIAG : Line, coords = ");

    cp = l->point;
    while(cp != NULL)
        {
        printf("%d,%d ", cp->point.x, cp->point.y);
        cp = cp->next;
        }
    printf("\n");
}

void    prt_poly(p)
poly_t *p;
{
cpoint_t    *cp;

    printf("DIAG : Poly, coords = ");
```

```
    cp = p->point;
    while(cp != NULL)
        {
        printf("%d,%d ",cp->point.x, cp->point.y);
        cp = cp->next;
        }
    printf("\n");
}


void    prt_text(t)
text_t  *t;
{
    printf("DIAG : Text [%s], at %d, %d with %c, %c\n",
        t->text, t->origin.x, t->origin.y, t->just[0], t->just[1]);
}


void    prt_ref(r)
ref_t   *r;
{
    printf("DIAG : Reference [%s] at  %d, %d\n",
        r->name, r->origin.x, r->origin.y);
}


void    prt_oval(r)
rect_t  *r;
{
    printf("DIAG : Oval left/bottom %d, %d right/top %d, %d\n",
        r->left, r->bottom, r->right, r->top);
}



void    prt_seg(seg)
seg_t   *seg;
{
key_t   *k;

    if(seg->name != NULL)
        printf("DIAG : Segment [%s]\n",seg->name);
    else
        printf("DIAG : Segment [No Name !!!]\n");
```

```c
    if(seg->bbox != NULL)
        {
        printf("\t\tExtent : ");
        prt_rect(seg->bbox);
        }


 k = seg->data;
 while(k != NULL)
        {
        switch(k->type)
            {
            /* primitives */
            case POINT   :    prt_point(k->key.point);          break;
            case LINE    :    prt_line(k->key.line);            break;
            case RECT    :    prt_rect(k->key.rect);            break;
            case TEXT    :    prt_text(k->key.text);            break;
            case REF     :    prt_ref(k->key.ref);              break;
            case POLY    :    prt_poly(k->key.poly);            break;
            case OVAL    :    prt_oval(k->key.oval);            break;


            /* attributes */
            case RESET   :    printf("%s RESET\n", mess);                   break;
            case COPY    :    printf("%s Draw mode COPY\n", mess);          break;
            case XOR     :    printf("%s Draw mode XOR\n", mess);           break;
            case FILL    :    printf("%s FILL\n", mess);                    break;
            case NOFILL  :    printf("%s NOFILL\n", mess);                  break;
            case FRAME   :    printf("%s FRAME\n", mess);                   break;
            case NOFRAME :    printf("%s NOFRAME\n", mess);                 break;
            case BLACK   :    printf("%s BLACK\n", mess);                   break;
            case WHITE   :    printf("%s WHITE\n", mess);                   break;
            case RED     :    printf("%s RED\n", mess);                     break;
            case GREEN   :    printf("%s GREEN\n", mess);                   break;
            case BLUE    :    printf("%s BLUE\n", mess);                    break;
            case CYAN    :    printf("%s CYAN\n", mess);                    break;
            case MAGENTA :    printf("%s MAGENTA\n", mess);                 break;
            case YELLOW  :    printf("%s YELLOW\n", mess);                  break;
            }

        k = k->next;
        }
}
```

draw.c

```
/*
    draw.c

    Segment and Key Drawing routines
*/

#include    "defs.h"

/* Internal state vars */
int    wr_mode   = COPY;
int    fill_mode = NOFILL;
int    frame_mode = FRAME;
int    fg_clr    = WHITE;

/* Display Size */
rect_t    screen;

/* current window and view port */
rect_t *cur_win    =    NULL;
rect_t *cur_port    =    NULL;

void    list_draw(key, viewport)
key_t    *key;
vport_t *viewport;
{
void    key_draw();

    if(viewport == NULL)
        {
        error("Segment viewport undefined in list_draw");
        return;
        }
    cur_port = viewport->bitmap;
    cur_win = viewport->window;

    re_map(cur_win, cur_port);
    set_map(cur_win, cur_port);

    while(key != NULL)
        {
        key_draw(key, viewport);
        key = key->next;
        }
}
```

```
void    key_draw(key, viewport)
key_t   *key;
vport_t *viewport;
{
void    draw_line(), frame_rect(), frame_poly();

    if(ISATTR(key->type))
        {
        switch(key->type)
            {
            case    RESET   :    /* reset to initial state */
                wr_mode = COPY;
                fill_mode = NOFILL;
                frame_mode = FRAME;
                fg_clr = WHITE;
                set_color(fg_clr);
                break;

            case    COPY    :    wr_mode = COPY;        break;
            case    XOR     :    wr_mode = XOR;         break;

            case    FILL    :    fill_mode = FILL;      break;
            case    NOFILL  :    fill_mode = NOFILL;    break;

            case    FRAME   :    frame_mode = FRAME;    break;
            case    NOFRAME :    frame_mode = NOFRAME;  break;

            default         :    fg_clr = key->type;
                set_color(fg_clr);
            }
        }
    else if(ISPRIM(key->type))
        {
        switch(key->type)
            {
            case    POINT   :
                {
                point_t *p;  p = key->key.point;
                move_to(p->x,  p->y);
                line_to(p->x,  p->y);
                break;
                }
```

```
case    LINE   :
    {
    line_t  *l;  l = key->key.line;
    draw_line(l);
    break;
    }
case    RECT   :
    {
    rect_t  *r;  r = key->key.rect;

    if(fill_mode == FILL)
        fill_rect(r);

    if(frame_mode == FRAME)
        frame_rect(r);
    break;
    }
case    TEXT   :
    {
    text_t  *t;  t = key->key.text;
    draw_text(t->text, t->origin.x, t->origin.y, t->bbox);
    break;
    }
case    REF    :
    {
    ref_t   *r;
    seg_t   *rd_seg();
    rect_t  *mf_bbox(), *copy_rect();
    r = key->key.ref;

    /* does the ref exist */
    if(r->instance == NULL)
        {
        r->instance = rd_seg(r->name);
        instance(r->instance);
        }

    /* did we read the metafile ? */
    if(r->instance != NULL)
        {
        vport_t vp;
```

```
                    vp.window = copy_rect(viewport->window);
                    vp.bitmap = viewport->bitmap;
                    vp.seg = r->instance;
                    vp.brder = viewport->brder;
                    vp.bkgnd = viewport->bkgnd;

            offset_rect(vp.window, -r->origin.x, -r->origin.y);
            draw_seg(r->instance, &vp);

            free(vp.window);

            cur_port = viewport->bitmap;
            cur_win = viewport->window;

            set_map(cur_win, cur_port);
            }

        break;
        }
    case    POLY    :
        {
        poly_t *p; p = key->key.poly;

        if(fill_mode == FILL)
            fill_poly(p);
        if(frame_mode == FRAME)
            frame_poly(p);
        break;
        }
    case    OVAL    :
        {
        oval_t *o; o = key->key.oval;

        if(fill_mode == FILL)
            fill_oval(o);
        if(frame_mode == FRAME)
            frame_oval(o);
        break;
        }
```

```
                              default :
                                   error("Unknown key type in keydraw");
                              }
                        }
            }


      /* rectangle intersection result */
      rect_t  r;

      void    draw_line(l)
      line_t  *l;
      {
      cpoint_t    *cp;

           if(sect_rect( l->bbox, cur_win, &r))
                 {
                 cp = l->point;
                 move_to(cp->point.x, cp->point.y);
                 while(cp != NULL)
                       {
                       line_to(cp->point.x, cp->point.y);
                       cp = cp->next;
                       }
                 }
      }


      void    frame_rect(rect)
      rect_t  *rect;
      {
           move_to(rect->left,  rect->bottom);
           line_to(rect->left,  rect->top);
           line_to(rect->right, rect->top);
           line_to(rect->right, rect->bottom);
           line_to(rect->left,  rect->bottom);
      }


      void    frame_poly(p)
      poly_t  *p;
      {
      cpoint_t    *cp;
```

```
    if(sect_rect( p->bbox, cur_win, &r))
        {
        cp = p->point;
        move_to(cp->point.x, cp->point.y);
        while(cp != NULL)
            {
            line_to(cp->point.x, cp->point.y);
            cp = cp->next;
            }
        }
}
```

file.c

```
/*
    file.c

    segment and metafile disk storage and retrieval routines
*/

#include     "defs.h"
#undef        NULL
#include     <stdio.h>

static  int         key_size = sizeof(disk_key_t);
static  disk_key_t  dkey;      /* key buffer for file i/o */

/* key primitive read buffers */
static  point_t   *pt;
static  line_t    *ln;
static  rect_t    *rt;
static  poly_t    *py;
static  oval_t    *ov;
static  text_t    *tx;
static  ref_t     *rf;

extern  seg_t   *top_seg;
extern  seg_t   *cur_seg;
```

```
seg_t    *rd_seg(name)
char     *name;
{
seg_t    *seg, *cl_seg(), *inst_seg();
key_t    *read_list();
rect_t   *get_bbox(), *copy_rect();
FILE     *fp;

    /* Does segment already exist? */
    seg = top_seg;
    while(seg != NULL)
        {
        if(seg->name != NULL)
            if(strcmp(seg->name, name) == 0)
                return(seg);

        seg = seg->next;
        }

    fp = fopen(name, "r");
    if(fp == NULL)
        {
        error("Can't open metafile, from read segment");
        return(NULL);
        }

    /* get an empty segment */
    seg = inst_seg(name);
    if(top_seg == NULL)
        {
        top_seg = seg;
        }
    else
        {
        seg->next = top_seg;
        top_seg = seg;
        }

    /* read the metafile */

    read_key(fp);     /* rt now contains bbox */
    seg->bbox = rt;
```

```
    seg->data = read_list(fp);

    /* set segment's initial stuff */
    seg->name = name;
    seg->visible = TRUE;
    seg->locked = FALSE;

    fclose(fp);
    return(seg);
}

key_t   *read_metafile(name)
char    *name;
{
key_t   *k;
key_t   *read_list();
FILE    *fp;
char    str[128];

    fp = fopen(name, "r");

    if(fp == NULL)
        {
        sprintf(str, "Can't open metafile %s", name);
        error(str);
        return(NULL);
        }

    read_key(fp);     /* rt now contains bbox */

    k = read_list(fp);
    fclose(fp);

    return(k);
}

rect_t *mf_bbox(name)
char    *name;
{
FILE    *fp;
char    str[128];

    fp = fopen(name, "r");
```

```
        if(fp == NULL)
            {
            sprintf(str,"Can't open metafile %s",name);
            error(str);
            return(NULL);
            }

        read_key(fp);       /* rt now contains bbox */
        fclose(fp);
        return(rt);
}

key_t    *read_list(fp)
FILE     *fp;
{
key_t    *k;
seg_t    seg;

        seg.data = NULL;
        op_seg(&seg);

        while(read_key(fp))
            switch(dkey.type)
                {
                case    POINT   :
                    add_point(pt);
                    break;
                case    LINE    :
                    add_line(ln);
                    break;
                case    RECT    :
                    add_rect(rt);
                    break;
                case    POLY    :
                    add_poly(py);
                    break;
                case    OVAL    :
                    add_oval(ov);
                    break;
                case    TEXT    :
                    add_text(tx);
                    break;
```

```
                case    REF    :
                    add_ref(rf);
                    break;
                default   :
                    add_attr(dkey. type);
                }


    cl_seg();
    return(seg. data);
}


static  int    read_key(fp)
FILE    *fp;
{
int     read_val, i;
line_t  *myline, *end_line();
poly_t  *mypoly, *end_poly();
key_t   *read_list();
point_t vpt;

    if((read_val = fread(&dkey, key_size, 1, fp)) == NULL)
        return(NULL);
    else
        {
        switch(dkey. type)
            {
            case    POINT    :
                pt = inst_point();
                fread(pt, sizeof(point_t), 1, fp);
                break;

            case    LINE    :
                ln = CALLOC(1,  line_t);
                if(ln == NULL)
                    error("Can't instantiate line");
                fread(ln, sizeof(line_t), 1, fp);
                i = ln->num_points;
                begin_line();
                while(i--)
                    {
                    fread(&vpt,  sizeof(point_t),  1,  fp);
                    con_point(vpt. x,  vpt. y);
                    }
```

```
            myline = end_line();
            ln->point = myline->point;
            break;

    case    RECT    :
            rt = inst_rect();
            fread(rt, sizeof(rect_t), 1, fp);
            break;

    case    POLY    :
            py = CALLOC(1,  poly_t);
            if(py == NULL)
                error("Can't instantiate poly");
            fread(py, sizeof(poly_t), 1, fp);
            i = py->num_points;
            begin_poly();
            while(i--)
                {
                fread(&vpt, sizeof(point_t), 1, fp);
                con_point(vpt.x,  vpt.y);
                }
            mypoly = end_poly();
            py->point = mypoly->point;
            break;

    case    OVAL    :
            ov = inst_oval();
            fread(ov,  sizeof(oval_t), 1, fp);
            break;

    case    TEXT    :
            tx = inst_text("");
            fread(tx,  sizeof(text_t), 1, fp);
            break;

    case    REF     :
            rf = inst_ref("", Ø, Ø, NULL);
            fread(rf, sizeof(ref_t), 1, fp);
            /*
                referenced segments are
                    read from disk when needed
            */
            break;
```

```
                default    :
                    {
                    /* must have been an attribute */
                    }
                }
            return(read_val);
            }
    }

void    wr_seg(seg)
seg_t   *seg;
{
void    write_metafile();

    if(seg->name == NULL)
        {
        error("Can't write an unnamed segment");
        return;
        }

    write_metafile(seg->name, seg->data, seg->bbox);
}

void    write_metafile(name, key, bbox)
char    *name;
key_t   *key;
rect_t  *bbox;
{
key_t   *k;
FILE    *fp;
char    str[128];

    fp = fopen(name, "w");

    if(fp == NULL)
        {
        sprintf(str, "Can't create metafile %s", name);
        error(str);
        return;
        }
```

```
    /* write bbox */
    dkey.type = RECT;
    dkey.size =      sizeof(rect_t);
    fwrite(&dkey, key_size, 1, fp);
    fwrite(bbox, dkey.size, 1, fp);

    k = key;
    while(k != NULL)
        {
        write_key(k, fp);
        k = k->next;
        }
    fclose(fp);
}

static   int     write_key(key, fp)
key_t    *key;
FILE     *fp;
{
int      i, j;

    dkey.type = key->type;
    switch(key->type)
        {
        case    POINT     :
            {
            point_t     *p;

            dkey.size = sizeof(point_t);
            fwrite(&dkey, key_size, 1, fp);
            p = key->key.point;
            fwrite(p, dkey.size, 1, fp);
            break;
            }
        case    LINE      :
            {
            line_t      *l;
            cpoint_t  *cpt;
            point_t    p;
```

```
    l = key->key.line;
    dkey.size = sizeof(line_t) + l->num_points * sizeof(point_t);
    fwrite(&dkey, key_size, 1, fp);
    fwrite(l, sizeof(line_t), 1, fp);
    cpt = l->point;
    while(cpt != NULL)
        {
        p.x = cpt->point.x;
        p.y = cpt->point.y;
        fwrite(&p, sizeof(point_t), 1, fp);
        cpt = cpt->next;
        }
    break;
    }
case    RECT    :
    {
    rect_t    *r;

    dkey.size =    sizeof(rect_t);
    fwrite(&dkey, key_size, 1, fp);
    r = key->key.rect;
    fwrite(r, dkey.size, 1, fp);
    break;
    }
case    POLY    :
    {
    poly_t    *pg;
    cpoint_t  *cpt;
    point_t   p;
    pg = key->key.poly;
    dkey.size = sizeof(poly_t) + pg->num_points * sizeof(point_t);
    fwrite(&dkey, key_size, 1, fp);
    fwrite(pg, sizeof(poly_t), 1, fp);
    cpt = pg->point;
    while(cpt != NULL)
        {
        p.x = cpt->point.x;
        p.y = cpt->point.y;
        fwrite(&p, sizeof(point_t), 1, fp);
        cpt = cpt->next;
        }
    break;
    }
```

```
            case    OVAL    :
                {
                oval_t    *o;

                dkey.size = sizeof(oval_t);
                fwrite(&dkey, key_size, 1, fp);
                o = key->key.oval;
                fwrite(o, dkey.size, 1, fp);
                break;
                }
            case    TEXT    :
                {
                text_t    *t;

                dkey.size =     sizeof(text_t);
                fwrite(&dkey, key_size, 1, fp);
                t = key->key.text;
                t->bbox = NULL;
                fwrite(t, dkey.size, 1, fp);
                break;
                }
            case    REF        :
                {
                ref_t    *r;
                dkey.size = sizeof(ref_t);
                fwrite(&dkey, key_size, 1, fp);
                r = key->key.ref;
                r->instance = NULL;
                fwrite(r, dkey.size, 1, fp);
                break;
                }
            default    :
                {
                dkey.size = 0;
                fwrite(&dkey, key_size, 1, fp);
                }
            }
    }
```

graphics.c

```
/*
    graphics.c

    device-dependent code
```

```
    NOTE:

        All routines in this file are passed
        world coordinates.

        These coordinates are operated on in the following order:

        1. clip-to-window     (world coordinates)
        2. map-to-viewport    (display coordinates)
        3. draw on display

*/

#include "defs.h"

extern rect_t  screen, *cur_win, *cur_port;

/* current position in window */
int cx = 0, cy = 0;

/* results of line clip */
extern int rx1, ry1, rx2, ry2;


/*

    display initialization, control, and
    termination subroutines

    initialize:
        erase display (to black),
        set up a color lookup table if needed,
        perform anything else

    set_color:
        takes attribute color as argument,
        sets current display draw color

    terminate:
        restore state of display to
        what it was before initialization
```

```
*/

void    initialize()
{
void    set_color();
/*
    set_rect(&screen, ...... );
*/
    set_color(WHITE);
}

void    set_color(attr)
int attr;
{
    switch(attr)
        {
        case BLACK  :    /* set display's equivalent color code */
        case WHITE  :
        case RED    :
        case GREEN  :
        case BLUE   :
        case MAGENTA :
        case CYAN   :
        case YELLOW :
            break;
        }
}

void    terminate()
{
}

/*

    simple movement and line drawing

*/
```

```
void     move_to(x, y)
int      x, y;
{
    printf("WC : Move to %d, %d\n", x, y);

    cx = x;
    cy = y;
}

void     move(x, y)
int      x, y;
{
    printf("WC : Move %d, %d\n", x, y);

    cx += x;
    cy += y;
}

void     line_to(x, y)
int      x, y;
{
    printf("WC : Line to %d, %d\n", x, y);

    if(clipper(cx, cy, x, y, cur_win))
        {
        map(&rx1, &ry1);
        map(&rx2, &ry2);

    printf("SC : Line %d, %d to %d, %d\n", rx1, ry1, rx2, ry2);
/*
        draw line from rx1, ry1 to rx2, ry2
*/
        }

    cx = x;
    cy = y;
}

void     line(x, y)
int  x, y;
{
    printf("WC : Line %d, %d\n", x, y);
```

```
    if(clipper(cx, cy, cx + x, cy + y, cur_win))
        {
        map(&rx1, &ry1);
        map(&rx2, &ry2);

    printf("SC : Line %d, %d to %d, %d\n", rx1, ry1, rx2, ry2);
/*
        draw line from rx1, ry1 to rx2, ry2
*/
        }

    cx += x;
    cy += y;
}

/*

    text routines:

    text_bbox returns rectangle that
    represents bounding box of text
    primitive

    draw_text draws given text on
    display in specified format

*/

rect_t  *text_bbox(string, jh, jv)
char    *string;
char    jh, jv;
{
rect_t  *bbox,
        *inst_rect();
int     offset;
int     size[2];    /* used to get bbox */

    printf("Text bbox\n");
    /* use system to find text bbox here */

    /* reset to system's text bbox */
    bbox = inst_rect( 0, 0, size[0], size[1]);
```

```
    /* offset for justification */
    switch(jh)
        {
        case    MIDDLE  :
            offset = 0 - size[0] / 2;
            offset_rect(bbox, offset, 0);
            break;
        case    RIGHT   :
            offset = 0 - size[0];
            offset_rect(bbox, offset, 0);
            break;
        }
    switch(jv)
        {
        case    CENTER  :
            offset =  0 - size[1] / 2;
            offset_rect(bbox, 0, offset);
            break;
        case    TOP :
            offset = 0 - size[1];
            offset_rect(bbox, 0, offset);
        }

    return(bbox);
}

void    draw_text(string, x, y, bbox)
char    *string;
int     x, y;
rect_t  *bbox;
{
rect_t  vbb;
char    str[256];

    printf("Draw text [%s] at %d, %d\n", string, x, y);

    /* copy string to scratch */
    strcpy(str, string);

    vbb.left = bbox->left + x;
    vbb.bottom = bbox->bottom + y;
```

```
    vbb.right = bbox->right + x;
    vbb.top = bbox->top + y;

    /* map viewable bbox */
    map( &(vbb.left), &(vbb.bottom));
    map( &(vbb.right), &(vbb.top));

    /* if hardware origin is at lower left */
    x = vbb.left;
    y = vbb.bottom;

    /* call system to draw text at x, y */

}

/*

    remaining routines fill and
    frame simple shapes
*/

void    fill_rect(rect)
rect_t *rect;
{
rect_t  r;

    printf("Fill rect %d, %d <-> %d, %d\n",
        rect->left, rect->bottom, rect->right, rect->top);

    if(sect_rect(rect, cur_win, &r))
        {
        printf("\tCC %d, %d <-> %d, %d\n", r.left, r.bottom, r.right, r.top);

        map( &(r.left),  &(r.bottom));
        map( &(r.right), &(r.top));

        printf("\tSC %d, %d <-> %d, %d\n", r.left, r.bottom, r.right, r.top);
/*
        draw primitive according to its color
*/
        }
}
```

```
void    clear_vport(vp)
vport_t *vp;
{
}


void    fill_oval(rect)
rect_t  *rect;
{
rect_t  r;

    printf("Fill oval %d, %d <-> %d, %d\n",
        rect->left, rect->bottom, rect->right, rect->top);

    if(sect_rect(rect, cur_win, &r))
        {
        map( &(r.left),  &(r.bottom));
        map( &(r.right), &(r.top));

        printf("\tSC %d, %d <-> %d, %d\n", r.left, r.bottom, r.right, r.top);
/*
        draw primitive according to its color
*/
        }
}

void    frame_oval(rect)
rect_t  *rect;
{
rect_t  r;

    printf("Frame oval %d, %d <-> %d, %d\n",
        rect->left, rect->bottom, rect->right, rect->top);

    if(sect_rect(rect, cur_win, &r))
        {
        map( &(r.left),  &(r.bottom));
        map( &(r.right), &(r.top));
```

```
        printf("\tSC %d, %d <-> %d, %d\n", r.left, r.bottom, r.right, r.top);
/*
        draw primitive according to its color

*/
        }

}


void    fill_poly(p)
poly_t  *p;
{
    printf("Fill Poly\n");

/*

        clip polygon to current window,
        map each of polygon's vertices,
        draw primitive according to its color

*/
}
```

inst.c

```
/*
    inst.c

    dynamic structure instantiation and de-allocation subroutines
*/

#include    "defs.h"

key_t   *inst_key()
{
key_t   *k;

    if(( k = CALLOC(1, key_t)) == NULL)
        {
        error("Can't instantiate key");
        return(NULL);
        }
    else
        return(k);
}
```

```
point_t    *inst_point(x, y)
int    x, y;
{
point_t    *p;

    if(( p = MALLOC(point_t)) == NULL)
        {
        error("Can't instantiate Point");
        return(NULL);
        }
    else
        {
        p->x = x;
        p->y = y;
        return(p);
        }
}

void    point(x, y)
int    x, y;
{
point_t    *p, *inst_point();

    p = inst_point(x, y);
    add_point(p);
}

rect_t    *inst_rect(left, bottom, right, top)
int    left, bottom, right, top;
{
rect_t    *r;

    if(( r = MALLOC(rect_t)) == NULL)
        {
        error("Can't instantiate Rectangle");
        return(NULL);
        }
```

```
    else
        {
        r->left = left;
        r->bottom = bottom;
        r->right = right;
        r->top = top;
        return(r);
        }
}

void    rect(left, bottom, right, top)
int     left, bottom, right, top;
{
rect_t    *r, *inst_rect();

    r = inst_rect(left, bottom, right, top);
    add_rect(r);
}

void    oval(left, bottom, right, top)
int     left, bottom, right, top;
{
rect_t    *r, *inst_rect();

    r = inst_rect(left, bottom, right, top);
    add_oval(r);
}


text_t *inst_text(text, x, y, jh, jv)
char    *text;
int     x, y;
char    jh, jv;
{
text_t    *t;

    if(( t = MALLOC(text_t)) == NULL)
        {
        error("Can't instantiate Text");
        return(NULL);
        }
```

```
    else
        {
        strncpy(t->text, text, TXTSZE);
        t->origin.x = x;
        t->origin.y = y;
        t->just[0] = jh;
        t->just[1] = jv;
        t->bbox = NULL;
        return(t);
        }
}

void    text(text, x, y, jh, jv)
char    *text;
int     x, y;
char    jh, jv;
{
text_t    *t, *inst_text();

    t = inst_text(text, x, y, jh, jv);
    add_text(t);
}


ref_t   *inst_ref(name, x, y, seg)
char    *name;
int      x, y;
seg_t    *seg;
{
ref_t    *r;

    if(( r = CALLOC(1,ref_t)) == NULL)
        {
        error("Can't instantiate reference");
        return(NULL);
        }
    else
        {
        strncpy(r->name, name, TXTSZE);
        r->origin.x = x;
        r->origin.y = y;
```

```
            if(seg != NULL)
                {
                r->instance = seg;
                instance(seg);
                }

        return(r);
        }
}

void    ref(name, x, y, seg)
char    *name;
int     x, y;
seg_t   *seg;
{
ref_t   *r, *inst_ref();

    r = inst_ref(name, x, y, seg);
    add_ref(r);
}

seg_t   *inst_seg(name)
char    *name;
{
seg_t   *s;

    /* use calloc to clear memory */

    if(( s = CALLOC(1, seg_t)) == NULL)
        {
        error("Can't instantiate segment");
        return(NULL);
        }
    else
        {
        s->name = name;
        return(s);
        }
}
```

map.c

```
/*

    map.c

    window-to-viewport mapping
*/

#include "defs.h"

extern  rect_t  screen;

static  double  sx, sy;
static  int     wx, wy, vx, vy, map_status;

void    set_map(window, bitmap)
rect_t  *window, *bitmap;
{
double  n, d;

    if(equal_rect(window, bitmap))
        {
        /* mapping not needed */
        map_status = 0;
        return;
        }

    map_status = 1;

    wx = window->left;
    wy = window->bottom;

    vx = bitmap->left;
    vy = bitmap->bottom;

    n = (double) (bitmap->right - bitmap->left);
    d = (double) (window->right - window->left);
    sx = n / d;

    n = (double) (bitmap->top - bitmap->bottom);
    d = (double) (window->top - window->bottom);
    sy = n / d;
}
```

```
void     map(x, y)
int *x, *y;
{
    if(map_status)
        {
        *x = vx + (int) (sx * (*x - wx));
        *y = vy + (int) (sy * (*y - wy));
        }
/*
    Many computer graphics systems have the bit map origin
    at the upper left of the display. This world coordinate
    system "assumes" that the origin is at the lower left.
    If your display coordinate origin is at the upper left,
    add the following line.
*/
    *y = screen.top - *y;
}


/*
    The default mapping algorithm "assumes" that the
    entire window will be mapped into the bit-map viewport.
    Because the aspect ratios of the viewport and window
    may be different, this operation causes distortion.
    To prevent distortion, adjust the window so that

        1. The window's aspect ratio matches the viewport.
        2. None of the original window data is lost.

    This adjustment is made by calling the following
    mapping function:

*/

void     re_map( window, bitmap )
rect_t *window, *bitmap;
{
double bx, by, wx, wy, bar, war;
coord    ave, new;
```

```
    /* calculate the aspect ratio for the bit-map viewport */
    bx = (double) ( bitmap->right - bitmap->left );
    by = (double) ( bitmap->top - bitmap->bottom );
    bar = bx / by;

    /* calculate the aspect ratio for the clip window */
    wy = (double) ( window->top - window->bottom );
    wx = (double) ( window->right - window->left );
    war = wx / wy;

    if( bar > war )
        {
        /* calculate new window half-width */
        new = (coord) ((wy * bx ) / ( by * 2.0 ));

        /* calculate average horizontal point */
        ave = ( window->left + window->right ) / 2;

        /* reset new horizontal width */
        window->left = ave - new;
        window->right = ave + new;
        }
    else
        {
        /* calculate new window half-height */
        new = (coord) ((wx * by ) / ( bx * 2.0 ));

        /* calculate average vertical point */
        ave = ( window->top + window->bottom ) / 2;

        /* reset new vertical height */
        window->top = ave + new;
        window->bottom = ave - new;
        }
}
```

seg.c

```
/*
    seg.c

    segment creation, edit, deletion, and control routines
*/

#include    "defs.h"
```

```
static  key_t  *top_key    =     NULL;
static  key_t  *cur_key    =     NULL;

seg_t   *top_seg   =     NULL;
seg_t   *cur_seg   =     NULL;

static  int opened = FALSE;

void    draw_seg(seg, vport)
seg_t   *seg;
vport_t *vport;
{
rect_t chk, *get_bbox(), *copy_rect();

    vport->seg = seg;
/*
    Check segment bbox to see if it's
    visible at all.
*/
    if(seg->visible && sect_rect(seg->bbox, vport->window, &chk))
        list_draw(seg->data, vport);
}

/* create segment */

BOOLEAN cr_seg(name)
char    *name;
{
seg_t   *seg, *inst_seg();

    if(opened != FALSE)
        {
        error("Can't create segment, please close current segment");
        return(FALSE);
        }
    else
        {
        opened = TRUE;

        /* get a new segment descriptor */
        seg = inst_seg(name);
        top_key = cur_key = NULL;
```

```
            /* link descriptor into segment list */
            if(top_seg == NULL)
                {
                top_seg = seg;
                }
            else
                {
                seg->next = top_seg;
                top_seg = seg;
                }

            /* track current segment */
            cur_seg = top_seg;

            return(TRUE);
            }
}

/* open segment */

BOOLEAN op_seg(seg)
seg_t    *seg;
{
    if(opened != NULL)
        {
        error("Can't open segment, please close current segment");
        return(FALSE);
        }
    else
        {
        opened = TRUE;
        cur_seg = seg;
        top_key = seg->data;
        cur_key = seg->eol;
        return(TRUE);
        }
}
```

```
/* append to current segment */

void    append(type, pointer)
int         type;
char    *pointer;
{
    if(opened == FALSE)
        return;

    if(top_key == NULL)
        {
        top_key = cur_key = inst_key();
        }
    else
        {
        cur_key->next = inst_key();
        cur_key = cur_key->next;
        }

    cur_key->key.ptr = pointer;
    cur_key->type = type;
}


/* close segment */

seg_t    *cl_seg()
{
rect_t *get_bbox();

    if(top_key == NULL)
        {
        error("Closing empty segment");
        return(NULL);
        }
    else
        {
        opened = FALSE;
        cur_seg->data = top_key;
        cur_seg->eol =  cur_key;
        top_key = cur_key = NULL;
```

```
        cur_seg->bbox = get_bbox(cur_seg->data);
        cur_seg->visible = TRUE;
        cur_seg->locked = FALSE;
        return(cur_seg);
        }
}


seg_t   *instance(seg)
seg_t   *seg;
{
    seg->num_inst++;
    return(seg);
}


void    del_seg(seg)
seg_t    *seg;
{
key_t   *next;
seg_t   *last;
void    free_key();

    if(seg->locked == TRUE)
        return;

    if(seg->num_inst == 0)
        {
        /* free segment data */
        cur_key = seg->data;
        while(cur_key != NULL)
            {
            next = cur_key->next;
            free_key(cur_key);
            cur_key = next;
            }

        /* free segment rectangles */
        if(seg->bbox != NULL)
            free(seg->bbox);
```

```
                    /* free segment descriptor */
                    if(top_seg == seg)
                        {
                        top_seg = seg->next;
                        free(seg);
                        return;
                        }
                    else
                        {
                        last = top_seg;
                        while(last->next != NULL)
                            {
                            if(last->next == seg)
                                {
                                /* patch segment list */
                                last->next = seg->next;
                                free(seg);
                                return;
                                }
                            last = last->next;
                            }
                        /* error: can't find segment */
                        }
                }
            else
                seg->num_inst--;
}

void    del_data(key)
key_t   *key;
{
seg_t   *seg;

    seg = top_seg;
    while(seg != NULL)
        {
        if(seg->data == key)
            {
            del_seg(seg);
            return;
            }
        seg = seg->next;
        }
}
```

```
void     free_key(key)
key_t    *key;
{
void     free_cpt();

    switch(key->type)
        {
        case    REF     :
            if(key->key.ref->instance != NULL)
                del_seg(key->key.ref->instance);
            break;

        case    LINE    :
            free_cpt(key->key.line->point);
            break;

        case    POLY    :
            free_cpt(key->key.poly->point);
            break;

        default :
                ;                       /* do nothing */
        }

    if(key->key.ptr != NULL)    /* if a primitive */
        free(key->key.ptr);

    free(key);
}

/* free links in continue point list */

void     free_cpt(cp)
cpoint_t    *cp;
{
    if(cp->next != NULL)
        free_cpt(cp->next);

    free(cp);
}
```

utils.c

```
/*
    utils.c
```

```
    support routines
*/


#include     "defs.h"
#undef       NULL
#include     "stdio.h"

void     error(string)
char     *string;
{
    printf("ERROR : %s\n", string);
}


#define max(a,b)     ((a) > (b) ? (a) : (b))
#define min(a,b)     ((a) < (b) ? (a) : (b))


/*
    point operations
*/

BOOLEAN pt_in_rect(r, pt)
rect_t  *r;
point_t *pt;
{
    if( (pt->x <= r->right) &&
        (pt->x >= r->left)  &&
        (pt->y <= r->top)   &&
        (pt->y >= r->bottom))
        return(TRUE);
    else
        return(FALSE);
}


BOOLEAN loc_in_rect(r, x, y)
rect_t  *r;
int     x, y;
{
    if( (x <= r->right) &&
        (x >= r->left)  &&
        (y <= r->top)   &&
        (y >= r->bottom))
        return(TRUE);
```

```
    else
        return(FALSE);
}


/*
    rectangle operations
*/

BOOLEAN equal_rect(a, b)
rect_t  *a, *b;
{
    if(a == b)
        return(TRUE);

    else if( (a->left == b->left) &&
             (a->right == b->right) &&
             (a->top == b->top) &&
             (a->bottom == b->bottom))
        return(TRUE);

    else
        return(FALSE);
}


BOOLEAN sect_rect(a, b, c)
rect_t    *a, *b, *c;
{
    if(a->top < b->bottom ||
       a->right < b->left ||
       a->bottom > b->top ||
       a->left > b->right)
        return(FALSE);
    else
        {
        c->left = max(a->left, b->left);
        c->bottom = max(a->bottom, b->bottom);
        c->right = min(a->right, b->right);
        c->top = min(a->top, b->top);
        return(TRUE);
        }
}
```

```
void    union_rect(a, b, c)
rect_t    *a, *b, *c;
{
    c->left = min(a->left, b->left);
    c->bottom = min(a->bottom, b->bottom);
    c->right = max(a->right, b->right);
    c->top = max(a->top,b->top);
}


rect_t *offset_rect(r, dh, dv)
rect_t *r;
int     dh, dv;
{
    r->left   += dh;
    r->bottom += dv;
    r->right  += dh;
    r->top    += dv;
    return(r);
}


rect_t  *inset_rect(r, dh, dv)
rect_t *r;
int     dh, dv;
{
    r->left   += dh;
    r->bottom += dv;
    r->right  -= dh;
    r->top    -= dv;
    return(r);
}

rect_t    *set_rect(r, left, bottom, right, top)
rect_t *r;
int    left, bottom, right, top;
{
    r->left  = left;
    r->bottom = bottom;
    r->right  = right;
    r->top    = top;
    return(r);
}
```

```
rect_t    *copy_rect(or)
rect_t *or;
{
rect_t *nr, *inst_rect();

    nr = inst_rect(or->left, or->bottom, or->right, or->top);
    return(nr);
}


/*
    get bounding box: scans segment's data,
    sets local bboxes (in primitives)
    and global bboxes (in references)
*/

rect_t    *get_bbox(key)
key_t     *key;
{
void    set_bbox();
rect_t *bbox, *kbb, *mf_bbox();
rect_t *new_bbox(), *text_bbox(), *get_bbox();
seg_t   *rd_seg();
cpoint_t *cpt;
text_t *tx;
ref_t  *rf;
poly_t *py;
line_t *ln;

    if(key == NULL)
        return(NULL);

    bbox = new_bbox();

    while(key != NULL)
        {
        switch(key->type)
            {
            case    POINT    :
                set_bbox(bbox, key->key.point->x,
                    key->key.point->y);
                break;
```

```
case    LINE    :
    ln = key->key. line;
    set_bbox(bbox, ln->bbox->left, ln->bbox->bottom);
    set_bbox(bbox, ln->bbox->right, ln->bbox->top);
    break;

case    OVAL    :
case    RECT    :
    set_bbox(bbox, key->key. rect->left,
        key->key. rect->bottom);

    set_bbox(bbox, key->key. rect->right,
        key->key. rect->top);
    break;

case    POLY    :
    py = key->key. poly;
    set_bbox(bbox,  py->bbox->left, py->bbox->bottom);
    set_bbox(bbox,  py->bbox->right, py->bbox->top);
    break;

case    TEXT    :
    tx = key->key. text;
    kbb = tx->bbox;
    if(kbb == NULL)
        tx->bbox = text_bbox(tx->text,  tx->just[0],  tx->just[1]);

    kbb = tx->bbox;
    if(kbb != NULL)
        {
        set_bbox(bbox, kbb->left + tx->origin. x,
            kbb->bottom + tx->origin. y);
        set_bbox(bbox, kbb->right + tx->origin. x,
            kbb->top + tx->origin. y);
        }
    break;

case    REF    :
    rf = key->key. ref;

    if(rf->instance == NULL)
        rf->instance = rd_seg(rf->name);
```

```
                    if(rf->instance != NULL)
                        {
                        kbb = rf->instance->bbox;
                        set_bbox(bbox, kbb->left + rf->origin.x,
                            kbb->bottom + rf->origin.y);
                        set_bbox(bbox, kbb->right + rf->origin.x,
                            kbb->top + rf->origin.y);
                        }
                    break;
                }

        key = key->next;
        }

    /* 1-bit border */
    inset_rect(bbox, -1, -1);
    return(bbox);
}

rect_t  *new_bbox()
{
rect_t  *bbox, *inst_rect();

    /* set initial bbox to unknown */
    bbox = inst_rect(BIG, BIG, NBIG, NBIG);
    return(bbox);
}

void    set_bbox(bbox, x, y)
rect_t  *bbox;
int     x, y;
{
    bbox->left =    min(bbox->left, x);
    bbox->bottom =  min(bbox->bottom, y);

    bbox->right =   max(bbox->right, x);
    bbox->top =     max(bbox->top, y);
}
```

view.c

```
/*
    view.c

    viewport creation and control routines
*/
```

```
#include "defs.h"

extern  rect_t  screen, *cur_win, *cur_port;

vport_t    *inst_vport()
{
vport_t    *vp;

    if(( vp = CALLOC(1, vport_t)) == NULL)
        {
        error("Can't instantiate viewport");
        return(NULL);
        }
    else
        return(vp);
}


vport_t *new_vport(bitmap)
rect_t  *bitmap;
{
vport_t *vp, *inst_vport();
rect_t  result, *copy_rect();

    vp = inst_vport();
    vp->brder = WHITE;
    vp->bkgnd = BLACK;

    cur_win = &screen;

    if(sect_rect(bitmap, &screen, &result) == FALSE)
        {
        error("Viewport not within bitmap");
        exit(0);
        }

    cur_port = vp->bitmap = copy_rect(&result);

    set_map(&screen, &screen);
    set_color(WHITE);
    frame_rect(bitmap);

    vp->window = NULL;
```

```
    bitmap->top--;
    bitmap->left++;
    return(vp);
}


void    set_vport_seg(vp, seg)
vport_t *vp;
seg_t   *seg;
{
rect_t *r, *copy_rect();

    vp->seg = seg;

    if(vp->window == NULL)
        vp->window = copy_rect(seg->bbox);
    else
        {
        r = seg->bbox;
        set_rect(vp->window, r->left, r->bottom, r->right, r->top);
        }
}


void    pan_vport(vp, dh, dv)
vport_t *vp;
int dh, dv;
{
    offset_rect(vp->window, -dh, -dv);
    if(vp->seg != NULL)
        {
        clear_vport(vp);
        draw_seg(vp->seg, vp);
        }
}

void    zoom_vport(vp, dh, dv)
vport_t *vp;
int dh, dv;
{
rect_t *w;
/* Do not let window get too small! */

    w = vp->window;
```

```
    if(w->left >= (w->right -2*dh))
        return;

    if(w->bottom >= (w->top - 2*dv))
        return;

    inset_rect(vp->window, dh, dv);
    if(vp->seg != NULL)
        {
        clear_vport(vp);
        draw_seg(vp->seg, vp);
        }
}
```

Appendix B
The User Interface Code

The following files comprise the source code for the user interface presented in Chapter 9, "Advanced User Interfaces: The System." This code consists of a single header file and four C source code files. Note: Since the user interface uses the segmentation system, the segmentation system must be compiled and linked before the user interface can be created. All user interface object files are linked together to form the user interface system file usrifsys. o. This object file is then linked with the segmentation system file segsys. o and the application file to create a binary program file. The following makefile may be used on UNIX™ systems to create the user interface system.

```
#Make file for user interface
OBJECTS = display.o event.o menu.o window.o
HEADERS = defs.h usrif.h

#executable binary file is called 'program,' application code 'main.c'
#assuming segsys.o file is up-to-date

program:        $(HEADERS) main.o segsys.o usrifsys.o
        cc $(LFLAGS) -o program main.o segsys.o usrifsys.o

usrifsys.o:        $(HEADERS) $(OBJECTS)
        ar r usrifsys.o $(OBJECTS)
        ranlib usrifsys.o

display.o:        $(HEADERS) display.c
        cc $(CFLAGS) -c display.c

event.o:        $(HEADERS) event.c
        cc $(CFLAGS)-c event.c
```

```
main. o:            $(HEADERS) main. c
        cc $(CFLAGS) -c main. c

menu. o:            $(HEADERS) menu. c
        cc $(CFLAGS) -c menu. c

window. o:          $(HEADERS) window. c
        cc $(CFLAGS) -c window. c

#end of makefile for user interface
```

usrif.h

```
/*
    usrif. h

    user interface header file
*/

#include "defs. h"

/* event manager type definitions */
#define NULL_EVENT          0
#define DN_BUTTON_EVENT     1
#define UP_BUTTON_EVENT     2
#define KEY_EVENT           3
#define ABORT_EVENT         4


struct  event_record
    {
    int     what;
    char    stroke;
    point_t where;
    };

typedef struct event_record event_t;
event_t *get_next_event();

/* window manager definitions */

struct  window_record
    {
    void (*key_fn)(),           /* window key function */
        (*button_fn)();         /* window button function */
```

```
    char    *name;
    seg_t   *shape, *data;
    rect_t  *data_win,
            *area,
            *title,
            *pane;

    struct  window_record *next, *prev;
    };

typedef struct window_record window_t;

#define MAX_WINDOWS 20

window_t    *what_window(),
            *front_window();

/* maximum number of menu items */
#define MAX_MENUS 16
```

main.c

```
/*
    main.c

    user interface demonstration file
*/

#include "usrif.h"
#undef   NULL
#include "stdio.h"

main(argc, argv)
int     argc;
char    *argv[];
{
event_t     *myevent;
window_t    *mywindow;
void        init_app();

    /* initialize segmentation system */
    initialize();
```

```
/* initialize event and window managers */
init_event();
init_window();

/* initialize application */
init_app();

/* enter event-driven user interface */
while(TRUE)
    {
    /* get an event */
    myevent = get_next_event();

    /* What kind of event was it? */
    switch( myevent->what )
        {
        case    NULL_EVENT :
            /* use this event for
                pseudobackground processes */
            break;

        case    ABORT_EVENT :
            /* interrupt! */
            break;

        case    KEY_EVENT    :

            /* In what window did the KEY_EVENT occur? */
            mywindow = what_window( &(myevent->where));

            if( mywindow == NULL)
                {
                /* must have been a desktop event */
                desktop( myevent);
                }
            else if( mywindow == front_window())
                {
                /* call key function */
                if( mywindow->key_fn != NULL)
                    (*(mywindow->key_fn))(myevent, mywindow);
                }
```

```
                    else
                        /* keypress in obscured window */
                        pop_window( mywindow);

                break;

            case    DN_BUTTON_EVENT :   /* button down */

                /* In what window did DN_BUTTON_EVENT occur? */
                mywindow = what_window( &(myevent->where));

                if( mywindow == NULL)
                    {
                    /* must have been a desktop event */
                    desktop( myevent);
                    }

                else if( mywindow == front_window())
                    {
                    if( in_title( &(myevent->where), mywindow))
                        /* call window-control function */
                        mod_window( myevent, mywindow);

                    else if( mywindow->button_fn != NULL)
                        /* call button function */
                        (*(mywindow->button_fn))(myevent, mywindow);
                    }
                else
                    /* button down in obscured window */
                    pop_window( mywindow);

                break;
            }

        }   /* loop forever */
    }

/*
    application test code
*/
```

```
#define WINDOWS 4
seg_t    *door, *window, *house;
window_t *them[WINDOWS];


void    init_app()
{
window_t *new_window();
seg_t    *cl_seg();

/*
    initialize application variables, windows, menu functions, etc.
*/

        cr_seg("window");
        add_attr(RESET);
        add_attr(BLACK);
        rect(10, 10, 60, 80);
        rect(10, 00, 60, 90);
        window = cl_seg();

        cr_seg("door");
        add_attr(RESET);
        add_attr(BLACK);
        rect(10, 0, 100, 170);
        door = cl_seg();

        cr_seg("house");

        add_attr(RESET);
        add_attr(BLACK);

        rect(100, 200, 600, 500);
        begin_line();
            con_point(50, 480);
            con_point(350, 600);
            con_point(650, 480);
        add_line(end_line());

        ref("window", 150, 300, NULL);
        ref("window", 250, 300, NULL);
        ref("window", 350, 300, NULL);

        ref("door", 450, 200, NULL);
```

```
        text("House",  0,  100,  LEFT ,  BOTTOM);

    house = cl_seg();

/*

    display house segment in four different windows
*/

    them[0] = new_window("Window 0", house, new_rect());
    them[1] = new_window("Window 1", house,
        inst_rect(150,  50, 300, 600));
    them[2] = new_window("Window 2", house, new_rect());
    them[3] = new_window("Window 3 is the last", house,
        inst_rect(100, 100, 600, 300));

/*

    return to event loop
*/
}
```

display.c

```
/*

    display.c

    miscellaneous display routines
*/

#include "usrif.h"
#undef   NULL
#include "ctype.h"
#include "stdio.h"

/*

    #include system-dependent header files here
*/

/* globals */
extern  rect_t  screen;
extern  vport_t *the_port;
```

```
/* desktop segment pointers */
seg_t   *desk_seg = NULL;
seg_t   *trash;

/* current and last cursor positions */
point_t cursor,
        last_loc;

int     erase = FALSE;

/* cursor operations */

/* set new cursor position */
void    set_cursor(loc)
point_t *loc;
{
    if(erase == FALSE)
        {
        erase = TRUE;
        last_loc.x = loc->x;
        last_loc.y = loc->y;
        xor_cursor(loc);
        }
    else if( (last_loc.x != loc->x) || (last_loc.y != loc->y) )
        {
        xor_cursor(&last_loc);
        last_loc.x = loc->x;
        last_loc.y = loc->y;
        xor_cursor(loc);
        }
    cursor.x = loc->x;
    cursor.y = screen.top - loc->y;
}

/* get current cursor position */
void    get_cursor( pt )
point_t *pt;
{
    if(pt == NULL)
        return;

    pt->x = cursor.x;
    pt->y = cursor.y;
}
```

```
/*
    cursor hide and show functions
*/

int view_status = FALSE;

void    hide_cursor()
{
    if(view_status == FALSE)
        {
        xor_cursor(&last_loc);
        erase = FALSE;
        }
    view_status++;
}

void    show_cursor()
{
    point_t loc;

    if(view_status == 1)
        {
        loc.x = cursor.x;
        loc.y = screen.top - cursor.y;
        set_cursor(&loc);
        }
    --view_status;
}

/*
    cursor drawing functions
*/

void    xor_cursor(loc)
point_t *loc;
{
/*
    exclusive OR the current cursor
    in the bit map at location 'loc'
*/
}
```

```c
/* desktop operations */

/* make desktop */
void    make_desktop()
{
    /* trash icon */
    cr_seg("trash");
        add_attr(RESET);
        add_attr(NOFILL);
        add_attr(BLACK);

        rect(7, 1, 25, 24);
        rect(6, 24, 26, 26);
        rect(13, 26, 19, 28);

        begin_line();
            con_point(10, 3);
            con_point(10, 22);
        add_line(end_line());

        begin_line();
            con_point(13, 3);
            con_point(13, 22);
        add_line(end_line());

        begin_line();
            con_point(19, 3);
            con_point(19, 22);
        add_line(end_line());

        begin_line();
            con_point(22, 3);
            con_point(22, 22);
        add_line(end_line());

        text("Trash", 16, 0, MIDDLE , TOP);
    trash = cl_seg();

    cr_seg("desk_top");
        add_attr(RESET);
```

```
        /* desktop background of white */
        add_attr(FILL);
        add_rect(&screen);
        ref("trash" , screen.right-70, 20, NULL);

    desk_seg = cl_seg();
}


#define CANCEL  0
#define PRINT   1
#define CLALL   2
#define QUIT    3

char    *desk_ops[4] =
    {
    "Cancel",
    "Print",
    "Close All",
    "Quit"
    };

void    desktop(event)
event_t    *event;
{
int sel;

    if(event->what == DN_BUTTON_EVENT)
        {
        sel = pop_up_menu( 4, desk_ops );

        switch(sel)
            {
            case  CANCEL : /* nothing */   break;
            case  PRINT  : print_screen(); break;
            case  CLALL  : purge_all();    break;
            case  QUIT   : exit();
            }
        }
    else if(event->what == KEY_EVENT)
        {
        /* perform desktop key function */
        }
}
```

event.c

```
/*

    event. c

    event manager routines and variables
*/

/*

    #include system-dependent header files here
*/

#include "usrif. h"
#undef   NULL
#include "ctype. h"
#include "stdio. h"

/* cursor record */
extern  point_t cursor;

/* keyboard lookup table */
char    key_map[256];

extern  rect_t  screen;

/* the event record */
event_t the_event;

/*

    initialize event manager
*/

void     init_event()
{
int i;

    /* initial cursor position */
    cursor. x = cursor. y = 0;

    /* default ascii keyboard lookup table */
    for(i=0; i<256; i++)
        if(isascii(i))
            key_map[i] = (char) i;
        else
            key_map[i] = '\0' ;
```

```
    /* initialize system-dependent event managers here */
}

event_t *get_next_event()
{
point_t where;
int     data;

    /* get system event */

    switch(type)    /* What type of event was it? */
        {
        case    /* no event */    :

            the_event.what = NULL_EVENT;
            break;

        case    /* button event */

            /* down button? */
                the_event.what = DN_BUTTON_EVENT;

            /* up button? */
                the_event.what = UP_BUTTON_EVENT;

            break;

        case    /* pointer moved */    :

            where.x = /* pointer x location */
            where.y = /* pointer y location */
            set_cursor( &where);

            /* movement of pointer is not event */
            the_event.what = NULL_EVENT;
            break;

        case    /* key was pressed */  :

            /* keyboard key is in data */

            the_event.stroke = key_map[data];
            the_event.what = KEY_EVENT;
```

```
                if(data == ABORT_KEY)
                    the_event.what = ABORT_EVENT;

            break;
        }

    /* set up the event record */
    the_event.where.x = cursor.x;
    the_event.where.y = cursor.y;

    return( &the_event );
}
```

menu.c

```
/*
    menu.c

    menu manager routines and variables
*/

#include "usrif.h"
#undef   NULL
#include "stdio.h"

/* global variables */
extern  rect_t  screen;
extern  vport_t *the_port;
extern  point_t cursor;

/* menu border in pixels */
#define BDR 3

/* menu text height in pixels */
#define TH 12

int     pop_up_menu( num_items, items)
int     num_items;
char    *items[];
{
```

```
char    *look, *animate_seg();
text_t  *t[MAX_MENUS];
rect_t  area, bmap;
rect_t  *bbox, *text_bbox();
int     i, h, w, mw = 0, x, y;
seg_t   *menu;
key_t   *key;
void    save_bitmap(), restore_bitmap();

    /* determine maximum item width */
    for(i=0; i<num_items; i++)
        {
        bbox = text_bbox(items[i],LEFT,BOTTOM);
        w = bbox->right -  bbox->left;
        free(bbox);

        if(w > mw)
            mw = w;
        }


    /* determine size of menu */
    h = (TH + 2*BDR) * num_items + 2;
    w = mw + 2*BDR;

    /* determine location of menu */
    x = cursor.x;     y = cursor.y;

    /* greater than left edge of screen? */
    if(x > (w/2 + BDR))
        x -= w/2;
    else
        x = w/2 + BDR;

    /* less than right edge of screen? */
    if( (x+w) > screen.right)
        x -= w + BDR;
    else
        x = screen.right - w - BDR;
```

```
/* greater than bottom edge of screen? */
if(y > (h/2 + BDR))
    y -= h/2;
else
    y = h/2 + BDR;

/* less than top edge of screen? */
if( (y+h) > screen.top)
    y -= h + BDR;
else
    y = screen.top - h - BDR;


set_rect(&area, x, y, x+w, y+h);
set_rect(&bmap, x-1, y-1, x+w+1, y+h+1);

cr_seg("menu");
    add_attr(RESET);
    add_attr(FILL);
    add_rect(copy_rect(&area));

    add_attr(NOFILL);
    add_attr(BLACK);
    add_rect(copy_rect(&area));

    for(i=0; i<num_items, i++)
        {
        t[i] = inst_text(items[i],
            x+2+w/2,  y+2*BDR+i*(TH + 2*BDR),
            MIDDLE, BOTTOM);

/*
        If you want menu items left-justified,
        use this text command:

        t[i] = inst_text(items[i],
            x+2*BDR,  y+2*BDR+i*(TH + 2*BDR),
            LEFT, BOTTOM);
*/

        add_text(t[i]);
        }
```

```
    menu = cl_seg();

    /* save bit-map region where menu goes */
    save_bitmap(&bmap);

    /* draw menu in bit map */
    hide_cursor();
    draw_seg(menu, the_port);

    /* re-adjust text bbox to world space */
    for(i=0; i<num_items; i++)
        {
        set_rect(t[i]->bbox,
            x+1, y+i*(TH+2*BDR) + 1,
            x-3+w, y+(i+1)*(TH+2*BDR))-2;
        }

    /* animate menu item selection */
    show_cursor();
    look = animate_seg(menu);
    del_seg(menu);

    /* replace bit-map region */
    restore_bitmap(&bmap);

    /* return selected item */
    for(i=0; i<num_items; i++)
        if(strcmp(look, items[i]) == 0)
            return(i);

    return(-1);
}

text_t *active = NULL;

char    *animate_seg(seg)
seg_t   *seg;
{
char    *item;
event_t *myevent;
key_t   *test;
text_t  *t;
```

```
for(;;)
    {
    myevent = get_next_event();

    if(myevent->what == UP_BUTTON_EVENT)
        {
        if(active == NULL)
            return(NULL);
        else
            {
            item = active->text;
            active = NULL;
            return(item);
            }
        }
    else if( pt_in_rect( seg->bbox, &(myevent->where) ))
        {
        test = seg->data;
        while(test != NULL)
            {
            /* is text primitive */
            if(test->type == TEXT)
                {
                t = test->key. text;
                if(pt_in_rect(t->bbox, &(myevent->where)))
                    {
                    if(active == NULL)
                        {
                        /* make t the active text */
                        xor_rect(t->bbox, FILL);
                        active = t;
                        }
                    else if(active != t)
                        {
                        /* dim old text, make t active */
                        xor_rect(active->bbox, FILL);
                        xor_rect(t->bbox, FILL);
                        active = t;
                        }
                    /* else do nothing */
                    }
                }
```

```
                    test = test->next;
                    }
                }
        /* must be outside menu area */
        else if(active != NULL)
            {
            xor_rect(active->bbox,FILL);
            active = NULL;
            }
        }
}

void    save_bitmap( rect )
rect_t  *rect;
{
    hide_cursor();

    /*
        save rectangular area of bit map
    */

    show_cursor();
}

void    restore_bitmap( rect )
rect_t  *rect;
{
    hide_cursor();

    /*
        restore rectangular area of bit map
    */

    show_cursor();
}

/*
    Instead of using the segmentation system's
    XOR feature, which clips and maps primitives,
    use this function to provide the fastest
    possible animation speed.
*/
```

```
xor_rect( rect, how)
rect_t  *rect;
int     how;
{

    swtich( how )
        {
        case FILL   :
            /*
                Xor FILLed rectangle
            */
            break;

        case FRAME  :
            /*
                Xor FRAMEd rectangle
            */
            break;
        }
}
```

window.c

```
/*
    window.c

    window manager functions and variables
*/

#include "usrif.h"
#undef   NULL
#include "stdio.h"

/* window management variables */
static  window_t  *front, *back;
int     num_windows = 0;

/* globals */
extern  seg_t   *desk_seg;
extern  rect_t  screen;
```

```
/* minimum window size */
#define MIN_WX  100
#define MIN_WY  70

/* viewport for window manager */
vport_t *the_port = NULL;

/* base rectangle for new_rect() */
rect_t  base_rect;

/* new window size */
#define HSIZE   400
#define VSIZE   300

/* offsets for new window */
#define HDEL    50
#define VDEL    50

#define VBASE   (screen.top-VSIZE-VDEL)
#define HBASE   HDEL

/* new window rectangle, offset variables */
int hdir = HDEL, vdir = 0-HDEL;

/*
    window manager initialization function

    init_window()
        called to reset window list,
        also creates and draws the
        desktop segment
*/

init_window()
{
vport_t *new_vport();

    front = back = NULL;
    num_windows = 0;

    /* make primary viewport */
    the_port = new_vport(&screen);
```

```
    /* map to entire screen */
    the_port->window = &screen;

    /* make desktop segment */
    make_desktop();
    draw_seg(desk_seg, the_port);

    /* set first window place and size */
    set_rect(&base_rect,
        HBASE, VBASE, HBASE+HSIZE, VBASE+VSIZE);
}


/*

    window creation functions

    new_window( name, segment, rect )
        instantiates a new window structure,
        creates the window shape segment
        to correspond with name and rect,
        links window into window list,
        draws new window,
        and returns a pointer to new window

    new_rect()
        creates new window rectangle,
        offset from last time
        new_rect() was called
*/

window_t    *new_window( name, segment, rect )
char        *name;
seg_t       *segment;
rect_t      *rect;
{
window_t    *new;
key_t       *mykey, *inst_key();
rect_t      *inst_rect(), *new_rect(), *copy_rect();
text_t      *inst_text();

void (view_window)();

    num_windows++;
    if(num_windows > MAX_WINDOWS)
        return(NULL);
```

```
if(new = CALLOC( 1, window_t))
    {
    new->name = name;

    /* check for minimum window size */
    if( (rect->right - rect->left) < MIN_WX)
        rect->right = rect->left + MIN_WX;

    if( (rect->top - rect->bottom) < MIN_WY)
        rect->top = rect->bottom + MIN_WY;

    /* get new window rectangle */
    new->area = rect;

    /* make title area rectangle */
    new->title = inst_rect(
        new->area->left + 2,
        new->area->top - 20,
        new->area->right - 2,
        new->area->top - 2);

    /* make data area rectangle */
    new->pane = inst_rect(
        new->area->left + 1,
        new->area->bottom + 1,
        new->area->right - 1,
        new->area->top - 22);

    /* make segment for window */
    cr_seg( name );
        add_attr(RESET);

        /* fill shape background */
        add_attr(FILL);
        add_rect(copy_rect(new->area));
        add_attr(NOFILL);

        /* frame shape background */
        add_attr(FRAME);
        add_attr(BLACK);
        add_rect(copy_rect(new->area));
```

```
            /* fill window title area */
            add_attr(FILL);
            add_attr(BLACK);
            add_rect(copy_rect(new->title));

            add_attr(WHITE);
            text(name,
                new->title->left + 8,
                new->title->bottom + 5,
                LEFT , BOTTOM);

        new->shape = cl_seg();

        new->data = segment;
        new->data_win = copy_rect(segment->bbox);

        draw_win( new );

        /* link to top of window list */
        /* no windows exist */
        if(front == NULL)
            back = front = new;

        /* some windows exist */
        else {
            /* make new window the front window */
            front->prev = new;
            new->next = front;

            new->prev = NULL;
            front = new;
            }
        }
    else
        error("can't create new window");

    /* set up window customer */
    new->button_fn = &view_window;
    return(new);
}
```

```
rect_t  *new_rect()
{
rect_t  r, *n, *copy_rect();
int p;

    /* copy current base window rectangle */
    n = copy_rect(&base_rect);

    offset_rect(&base_rect, hdir, vdir);

    /* move base rectangle to new position */
    if( base_rect.right > screen.right)
        {
        p = base_rect.bottom;
        set_rect(&base_rect, HBASE, p, HBASE+HSIZE, p+VSIZE);
        }

    if( base_rect.bottom < screen.bottom)
        {
        p = base_rect.left;
        set_rect(&base_rect, p, VBASE, p+HSIZE, VBASE+VSIZE);
        }

    return(n);
}

/*

    window pop function

    pop_window(window)
        makes given window the
        top, or active, window
*/


pop_window( window )
window_t    *window;
{
    /* already on top? */
    if(window == front)
        return;
```

```
    /* relink to top */
    if(window == back)
        {
        /* window is bottom one */
        window->prev->next = NULL;
        back = window->prev;
        }
    else  /* not front or back */
        {
        window->prev->next = window->next;
        window->next->prev = window->prev;
        }

    front->prev = window;
    window->next = front;

    window->prev = NULL;
    front = window;

  /* draw window */
    draw_win(window);
}

/*

    window detection functions

    front_window()
        returns window pointer to
        active, or front, window

    what_window( where )
        returns pointer to
        top window that the point
        where is in, else NULL

    in_window( point, window)
    in_title( point, window)
    in_pane( point, window)
        these return TRUE if point
        is in the region, else FALSE

*/
```

```
window_t    *front_window()
{
    return(front);
}


window_t    *what_window( where )
point_t     *where;
{
window_t    *mywin, *inwin;

    inwin = NULL;
    mywin = back;

    while(mywin != NULL)
        {
        if(in_window( where, mywin ))
            inwin = mywin;

        /* next higher window */
        mywin = mywin->prev;
        }

    return(inwin);
}

in_window( point, window)
point_t     *point;
window_t    *window;
{
    if(pt_in_rect( window->area, point))
        return(TRUE);

    return(FALSE);
}

in_title( point, window)
point_t     *point;
window_t    *window;
{
    if(pt_in_rect( window->title, point))
        return(TRUE);

    return(FALSE);
}
```

```
in_pane( point, window)
point_t      *point;
window_t     *window;
{
    if(pt_in_rect( window->pane, point))
        return(TRUE);

    return(FALSE);
}

/*
    window menu control functions

    mod_window( event, window )
        queries user for window modification
        for the active window, then performs
        selected modification operation

    view_window( event, window )
        queries user for view operation
        for active window, then performs
        selected view operation
*/

/* operation selection menu item definitions */
#define CANCEL  0
#define MOVE    1
#define SIZE    2
#define CLOSE   3

/* window modify operation selection menu items */
char    *mod_ops[4] =
    {
    "Cancel",
    "Move",
    "Size",
    "Close"
    };
```

```
mod_window( event, window )
event_t      *event;
window_t     *window;
{
int sel;
rect_t  *old_rect, *copy_rect();

    /* pops up menu, user selects item */
    sel = pop_up_menu( 4, mod_ops );

    /* which item was selected? */
    switch(sel)
        {
        case    CANCEL   :
            /* user decided not to modify */
            return;

        case    MOVE     :
            /* animate window move */
            {
            point_t first, last, delta;
            key_t   *key;

            /* copy window bounds */
            old_rect = copy_rect(window->area);

            get_cursor(&first);
            xor_rect(window->area, FRAME);

            /* animate window outline */
            while(event->what != DN_BUTTON_EVENT)
                {
                get_cursor(&last);
                event = get_next_event();

                delta.x = event->where.x - last.x;
                delta.y = event->where.y - last.y;

                if( delta.x != 0 || delta.y != 0)
                    {
                    /* remove old outline */
                    xor_rect(window->area, FRAME);
```

```
                    /* set new outline */
                    offset_rect(window->area, delta.x, delta.y);

                    /* add new outline */
                    xor_rect(window->area,FRAME);
                    }
                }

        /* found new window size */
        xor_rect(window->area,FRAME);

        /* calculate window's change in position */
        delta.x = event->where.x - first.x;
        delta.y = event->where.y - first.y;

        /* offset window's regions */
        offset_rect(window->title, delta.x, delta.y);
        offset_rect(window->pane, delta.x, delta.y);
        offset_rect(window->shape->bbox, delta.x, delta.y);

        /* offset window's shape segment */
        key = window->shape->data;

        while(key != NULL)
            {
            switch(key->type)
                {
                case RECT :
                    offset_rect(key->rect, delta.x, delta.y);
                    break;
                case TEXT :
                    key->text->origin.x += delta.x;
                    key->text->origin.y += delta.y;
                    break;
                }
            key = key->next;
            }

        /* refresh bit map */
        all_wins( old_rect );
        free(old_rect);
```

```
        draw_win( window );
        }
        break;

case    SIZE    :
    /* animate window sizing */
    {
    point_t first, last, delta;
    key_t   *key;

    /* copy window bounds */
    old_rect = copy_rect(window->area);

    first.x = window->area->right;
    first.y = screen.top - window->area->bottom;
    set_cursor(&first);

    first.y = window->area->bottom;

    xor_rect(window->area, FRAME);

    /* animate window outline */
    while(event->what != DN_BUTTON_EVENT)
        {
        get_cursor(&last);
        event = get_next_event();

        if(event->where.x < (window->area->left + MIN_WX))
            delta.x = 0;
        else
            delta.x = event->where.x - last.x;

        if(event->where.y > (window->area->top - MIN_WY))
            delta.y = 0;
        else
            delta.y = event->where.y - last.y;

        if( delta.x != 0 || delta.y != 0)
            {
            /* remove old outline */
            xor_rect(window->area, FRAME);
```

```
                    /* set new outline */
                    window->area->right += delta.x;
                    window->area->bottom += delta.y;

                    /* add new outline */
                    xor_rect(window->area, FRAME);
                    }
            }

    /* found new window size */
    xor_rect(window->area, FRAME);

    /* calculate window's change in position */
    delta.x = window->area->right - first.x;
    delta.y = window->area->bottom - first.y;

    /* offset window's regions */
    window->title->right += delta.x;

    window->pane->right += delta.x;
    window->pane->bottom += delta.y;

    window->shape->bbox->right += delta.x;
    window->shape->bbox->bottom += delta.y;

    /* redo window's shape segment
    to reflect new size */
    key = window->shape->data;

    while(key != NULL)
        {
        if(key->type == RECT)
            {
            if(key->rect->bottom == window->title->bottom)
                /* do not change title bottom */
                key->rect->right += delta.x;
```

```
                        else
                            {
                            key->rect->right += delta.x;
                            key->rect->bottom += delta.y;
                            }
                        }
                    key = key->next;
                    }

            /* refresh bit map */
            all_wins( old_rect );
            free(old_rect);

            draw_win( window );
            }
            break;

        case    CLOSE   :
            /* remove window */
            purge_window( window);

            /* refresh */
            all_wins( window->area );

            break;
        }

    /* refresh display */
}

/* window view operation selection menu items */

#define CANCEL  0
#define REDUCE  1
#define ENLARGE 2
#define SCROLL  3
#define FIT     4
```

```c
char     *view_ops[5] =
    {
    "Cancel",
    "Reduce",
    "Enlarge",
    "Scroll",
    "Fit"
    };

/* scroll operation types */
#define S_UP      0
#define S_LEFT    1
#define S_RIGHT   2
#define S_DOWN    3

char     *scroll_ops[4] =
    {
    "Up",
    "Left",
    "Right",
    "Down"
    };

void view_window(event, window)
event_t    *event;
window_t   *window;
{
int sel, zoom, pan, h, w;
rec_t  *copy_rect();

    /* pop up view modify menu, user selects item */
    sel = pop_up_menu( 5, view_ops );

    switch(sel)
        {
        case  CANCEL    :
            break;

        case  REDUCE    :
            h = window->data_win->right - window->data_win->left;
            w = window->data_win->top - window->data_win->bottom;
            zoom = h > w ? h/10 : w/10;
```

```
        inset_rect(window->data_win, -zoom, -zoom);
        draw_win(window);
        break;

case  ENLARGE   :
        h = window->data_win->right - window->data_win->left;
        w = window->data_win->top - window->data_win->bottom;
        zoom = h < w ? h/10 : w/10;

        inset_rect(window->data_win, zoom, zoom);
        draw_win(window);
        break;

case  SCROLL    :
        /* pop up scroll menu, user selects item */
        sel = pop_up_menu( 4, scroll_ops );

        h = window->data_win->right - window->data_win->left;
        w = window->data_win->top - window->data_win->bottom;

        switch(sel)
            {
            case     S_LEFT :
                pan = h / 3;
                offset_rect(window->data_win, pan, 0);
                break;

            case     S_RIGHT :
                pan = h / 3;
                offset_rect(window->data_win, -pan, 0);
                break;

            case     S_UP    :
                pan = w / 3;
                offset_rect(window->data_win, 0, -pan);
                break;

            case     S_DOWN  :
                pan = w / 3;
                offset_rect(window->data_win, 0, pan);
                break;
            }
```

```
                /* do scroll */
                draw_win( window );
                break;

         case  FIT        :
                free(window->data_win);
                window->data_win = copy_rect(window->data->bbox);
                draw_win(window);
                break;
         }
}


/*

    window drawing functions

    draw_win(window)
        draws given window

    draw_all()
        draws desktop, then all windows
        from back to front
*/

draw_win( window )
window_t *window;
{
vport_t winport;
rect_t  tr;

    union_rect(&screen, window->area, &tr);
    if( equal_rect(&screen, &tr) == FALSE)
        {
        win_inrect( window, window->area );
        return;
        }

    /* hide cursor */
    hide_cursor();

    /* draw window's shape segment */
    draw_seg(window->shape, the_port);
```

```
    if(window->data != NULL)
        {
        /* set up viewport for window's data segment */
        winport.bitmap = window->pane;
        winport.window = window->data_win;
        winport.seg = window->data;

        /* draw window's data segment */
        draw_seg(window->data, &winport);
        }

    /* show cursor */
    show_cursor();
}


draw_all()
{
window_t    *mywin;

    /* hide cursor */
    hide_cursor();
    draw_seg(desk_seg, the_port);

    mywin = back;
    while(mywin != NULL)
        {
        draw_win(mywin);

        /* next higher window */
        mywin = mywin->prev;
        }

    /* show cursor */
    show_cursor();
}

all_wins( inrect )
rect_t *inrect;
{
window_t    *mywin;
vport_t     winport;
```

```
    /* hide cursor */
    hide_cursor();

    /* add small border */
    inset_rect( inrect, -1, -1);

    winport.bitmap = inrect;
    winport.window = inrect;
    draw_seg( desk_seg, &winport);

    mywin = back;
    while(mywin != NULL)
        {
        win_inrect( mywin, inrect );
        /* next higher window */
        mywin = mywin->prev;
        }

    inset_rect(inrect, 1, 1);

    /* show cursor */
    show_cursor();
}

/*
    refresh window in rectangle
*/

win_inrect( window, rect )
window_t    *window;
rect_t      *rect;
{
vport_t winport;
double  nl, nb, nr, nt, /* normalized display coordinates */
        pw, ph;          /* width and height */
rect_t  sr, pr, wr, tpr, twr;   /* screen, port, and window rect */
rect_t *copy_rect();

    /* hide cursor */
    hide_cursor();

    /* clip draw rect to screen */
    sect_rect(&screen, rect, &sr);
```

```
    /* set up viewport for window's data segment */
    winport.bitmap = copy_rect(&sr);
    offset_rect(winport.bitmap, -1, 0);
    winport.window = &sr;

    /* draw window's shape segment */
    draw_seg(window->shape, &winport);

    free(winport.bitmap);

    if(window->data != NULL)
        {
        if(clip_map( window->pane, window->data_win, &sr, &pr, &wr))
            {
            winport.bitmap = &pr;
            winport.window = &wr;

            /* draw window's data segment */
            draw_seg(window->data, &winport);
            }
        }

    /* show cursor */
    show_cursor();
}

/*
    clip map takes viewport bounds,
    clipping window, and clipping rectangle
    as arguments; then returns new
    viewport bounds and clipping window
*/

clip_map( old_port, old_win, clip_rect, new_port, new_win)
rect_t  *old_port,
        *old_win,
        *clip_rect,
        *new_port,
        *new_win;
{
double  nl, nb, nr, nt, /* normalized display coords */
        pw, ph;         /* width and height */
```

```
    if(sect_rect(clip_rect, old_port, new_port))
        {
        pw = (double) (old_port->right - old_port->left);
        ph = (double) (old_port->top - old_port->bottom);
        /* These must never be equal to 0.0! */

        /* convert clipped port to normalized display coordinates */
        nl = ((double) (new_port->left - old_port->left)) / pw;
        nr = ((double) (new_port->right - old_port->left)) / pw;

        nb = ((double) (new_port->bottom - old_port->bottom)) / ph;
        nt = ((double) (new_port->top - old_port->bottom)) / ph;

        /* find new window */
        pw = (double) (old_win->right - old_win->left);
        ph = (double) (old_win->top - old_win->bottom);

        if(nl == 0.0)
            new_win->left = old_win->left;
        else
            new_win->left = old_win->left + (int) ( nl * pw );

        if(nb == 0.0)
            new_win->bottom = old_win->bottom;
        else
            new_win->bottom = old_win->bottom + (int) ( nb * ph );

        if(nr == 1.0)
            new_win->right = old_win->right;
        else
            new_win->right = old_win->left + (int) ( nr * pw );

        if(nt == 1.0)
            new_win->top = old_win->top;
        else
            new_win->top = old_win->bottom + (int) ( nt * ph );

        return(TRUE);
        }
    else
        return(FALSE);
}
```

```
/*
    window removal functions

    purge_window(window)
        removes given window from
        linked window list

    purge_all()
        resets window list to be empty

    Note:
        both functions call draw_all()
*/

purge_window(window)
window_t    *window;
{
/*
    remove from doubly linked list
    remove window shape segment
    free window structure from memory

    Note:
        Only the front or active window
        can be purged.

        This does not free the window structure
        or its associated data from memory!
*/

    if(window == back)
        /* last window in list */
        front = back = NULL;
    else
        {
        front->next->prev = NULL;
        front = front->next;
        }

    window->next = window->prev = NULL;
    num_windows--;
}
```

```
purge_all()
{
/*
    remove all windows

    Note:
        This does not free window structures
        or their associated data from memory!
*/
    front = back = NULL;

    draw_all();
    num_windows = 0;
}
```

Appendix C

User Interface
Screen Images

The screen images in this appendix show what the user interface system looks like when operating. The file main.c in Appendix B provides the code (the sample application) from which the screen images were derived. Each screen image shows a particular function of the user interface. The images show the reader what the running code from Appendix B produces.

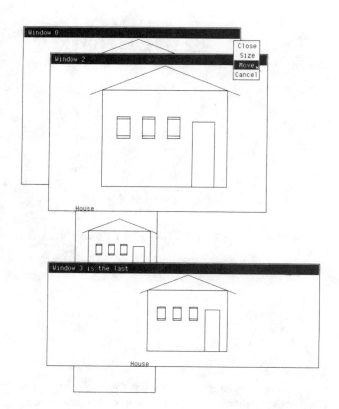

Fig. A. Window modification menu.

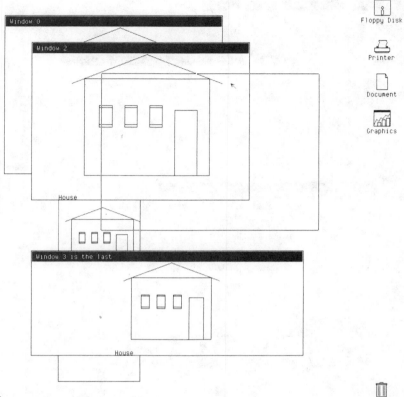

Fig. B. Window move operation.

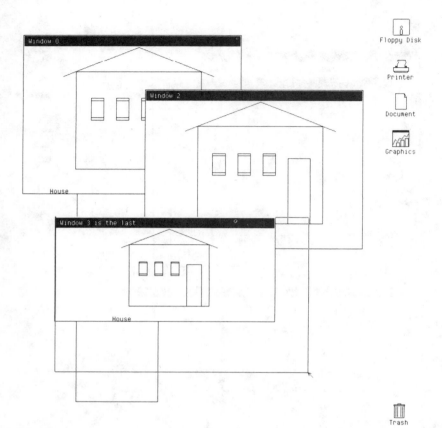

Fig. C. Window size operation.

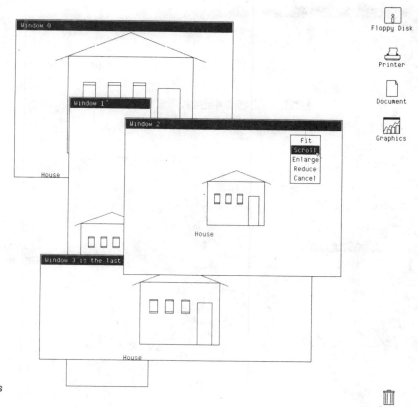

Fig. D. Window view operations menu.

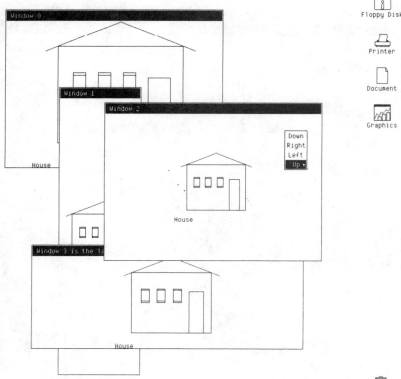

Fig. E. Window scroll menu.

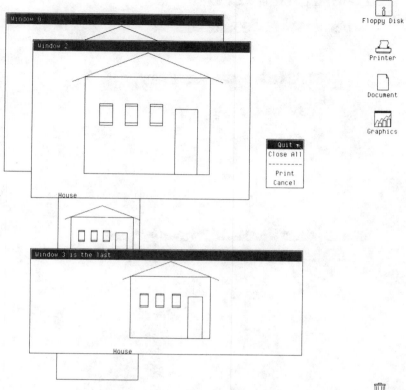

Floppy Disk

Printer

Document

Graphics

Trash

Fig. F. Desktop operations menu.

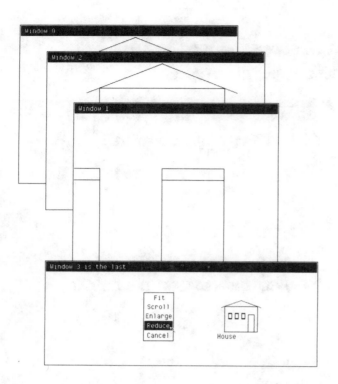

Fig. G. Data scaling.

Appendix D

IBM PC Graphics

The following code has been written with Computer Innovation's C86, Version 2.3, using the **-M** switch. The code provides the necessary graphics primitives for the IBM PC under DOS.

Version 2.3 of C86 implements distinct structure/union member names, using the **-M** switch. To compile this code, you must use Version 2.3 (or later) and the **-M** switch or make extensive changes to the structures in defs. h file.

This code can be adapted to other compilers. The major change is the 8086 interrupt call sysint( ). The form of sysint( ) is

```
int sysint(intnumber, inregs, outregs)
int intnumber;              /* the 8086 interrupt to perform */
struct regs inregs;         /* struct with info to load into 8086 */
struct regs outregs;        /* struct with info from 8086 */
```

The regs structure is shown at the top of the program file.

```
#include <stdio.h>
#include "defs.h"

static int CURx = 0, CURy = 0;  /* Current cursor location */

/* Structure for the c86 regs to be passed to sysint call */

typedef struct regs {
                int ax, bx, cx, dx, si, di, ds, es;
            } REG_ST;
```

```
static REG_ST reg1, reg2;
static char mode, page, color, colorb;
static int OVALF = 0;

extern int rx1, rx2, ry1, ry2;
extern rect_t screen, *cur_win, *cur_port;

#define abs(x)  ( ( x ) < 0 ? ( -x ) : ( x ) )

#define UP    1
#define DN    3
#define RT    4
#define LT   12
#define UPLT 13
#define UPRT  5
#define DNRT  7
#define DNLT 15


double do_d();
char get_move();

/*+1**********************************************************************/
/*                                                                      */
/*      initialize  -   Initializes the screen                          */
/*                                                                      */
/*      description -   Sets the color to white, sets the screen to 320 x 200 */
/*                      graphics,  draws a square around the screen, and sets  */
/*                      the global screen window                        */
/*                                                                      */
/*      parameters  -   initialize()                                    */
/*                                                                      */
/*      returns     -   NOTHING                                         */
/*                                                                      */
/*      Programmer  -   Jeff Wrench                                     */
/*                                                                      */
/*-1**********************************************************************/

initialize()
{
    CURx = CURy = 0;
    set_rect(&screen, 0, 0, 319, 199);          /* set global screen rectangle */
    cur_win = cur_port = &screen;
    reg1.ax = 0x0f00;                           /* get finish values for terminate */
```

```
    sysint(Øx1Ø, &reg1, &reg2);
    page = reg2.bx >> 8;                    /* monitor page to reset to */
    mode = reg2.ax;                         /* screen mode to reset to */
    reg1.ax = 4;
    sysint(Øx1Ø, &reg1, &reg2);             /* set to 320 x 200 color graph mode */
    set_color(WHITE);
    line_to(319, Ø);                        /* do screen rectangle */
    line_to(319, 199);
    line_to(Ø,   199);
    line_to(Ø,   Ø);
}


/*+1**************************************************************************/
/*                                                                          */
/*      set_color   -   set the draw color                                  */
/*                                                                          */
/*      description -   sets the glogal drawing color - CAUTION: Most of the */
/*                      eight colors use 2 pixels per color. This is in color */
/*                      graphics mode, the IBM only gives you 4 colors, so   */
/*                      I had to combine them in pairs to get all eight colors*/
/*                                                                          */
/*      parameters  -   get_color(col)                                      */
/*                      int col;         The color to be set to             */
/*                                                                          */
/*      Returns     -   Nothing                                            */
/*                                                                          */
/*      Programmer  -   Jeff Wrench                                         */
/*                                                                          */
/*-1**************************************************************************/

set_color(col)
int col;
{
    switch(col)
    {
        case BLACK  :   /* set display's equivalent color code */
                    color = Ø;
                    break;
        case WHITE  :
                    color = 15;
                    break;
        case RED    :
                    color = 2;
                    break;
```

```
        case GREEN   :
                     color = 5;
                     break;
        case BLUE    :
                     color = 8;
                     break;
        case MAGENTA :
                     color = 10;
                     break;
        case CYAN    :
                     color = 4;
                     break;
        case YELLOW  :
                     color = 3;
                     break;
    }
}


/*+1*****************************************************************************/
/*                                                                            */
/*      terminate   -   Reset the system                                      */
/*                                                                            */
/*      description -   reset the system to the way it was before the         */
/*                      initialize call                                       */
/*                                                                            */
/*      parameters  -   terminate()                                           */
/*                                                                            */
/*      returns     -   Nothing                                              */
/*                                                                            */
/*      Programmer  -   Jeff Wrench                                           */
/*                                                                            */
/*-1*****************************************************************************/

terminate()
{
    reg1.ax = mode;                    /* reset the mode */
    sysint(0x10, &reg1, &reg2);
    if ( page )                        /* if was on page other than 1 reset it */
    {
        reg1.ax = 0x500 | page;
        sysint(0x10, &reg1, &reg2);
    }
}
```

```
/*+1*******************************************************************************/
/*                                                                              */
/*      line        -    Draw a line                                            */
/*                                                                              */
/*      description -    Draws a line from the current location to the          */
/*                       location referenced by CURx + x, CURy + y.  It also    */
/*                       updated ( CURx, CURy ) to point to the end of the      */
/*                       line.                                                   */
/*                                                                              */
/*      parameters  -    line(x, y)                                             */
/*                       int x;             The Dx to move                      */
/*                       int y;             The Dy to move                      */
/*                                                                              */
/*      returns     -    Nothing                                                */
/*                                                                              */
/*      Programmer  -    Jeff Wrench                                            */
/*                                                                              */
/*-1*******************************************************************************/

line(x1, y1)
int     x1, y1;
{
int x2, y2;              /* The end point*/
int x, y;
int adx, ady;           /* The distance to move */
int xa, ya;             /* The direction to move */
int d;                  /* The distance already moved */
int incr1, incr2;       /* The distance moved each time */
int savx, savy;


    if ( clipper ( CURx, CURy, x1 + CURx, y1 + CURy, cur_win ) )
    {
        savx = rx2;
        savy = ry2;

        map ( &rx1, &ry1 );         /* map to screen coordinates */
        map ( &rx2, &ry2 );

        colorb = ( color >> 2 ) & 3;

        x = rx2 - rx1;
        y = ry2 - ry1;
```

```c
    if ( x < 0 )              /* Set up to move backward on the X-axis */
    {
        xa = -1;
        adx = -x;
    }
    else                      /* Set up to move forward on the X-axis */
    {
        xa =  1;
        adx =  x;
    }


    if ( y < 0 )              /* Set up to move backward on the Y-axis */
    {
        ya = -1;
        ady = -y;
    }
    else                      /* Set up to move forward on the Y-axis */
    {
        ya =  1;
        ady =  y;
    }


    if (adx > ady)        /* Are we moving more over than up */
    {
        incr1 = ady << 1;
        d = incr1 - adx;
        incr2 = incr1 - ( adx << 1 );
        while ( rx1 != rx2 )
        {
            rx1 += xa;
            if (d < 0)
                d += incr1;
            else
            {
                ry1 += ya;
                d += incr2;
            }
            CURx = rx1;
            CURy = ry1;
            do_pix();
        }
    }
```

```
        else                            /* Are we going more over than up */
        {
            incr1 = adx << 1;
            d = incr1 - ady;
            incr2 = incr1 - ( ady << 1 );
            while ( ry1 != ry2 )
            {
                ry1 += ya;
                if (d < 0)
                    d += incr1;
                else
                {
                    rx1 += xa;
                    d += incr2;
                }
                CURx = rx1;
                CURy = ry1;
                do_pix();
            }
        }

        CURx = savx;
        CURy = savy;
    }
}

/*+1*******************************************************************************/
/*                                                                              */
/*      line_to     -   Draw a line                                             */
/*                                                                              */
/*      description -   Draws a line from the current location to the           */
/*                      location referenced by ( x, y ).  It also updated       */
/*                      ( CURx, CURy ) to point to the end of the               */
/*                      line.                                                   */
/*                                                                              */
/*      parameters  -   line(x, y)                                              */
/*                      int x;          The Absolute position to move to        */
/*                      int y;          The Absolute position to move to        */
/*                                                                              */
/*      returns     -   Nothing                                                 */
/*                                                                              */
/*      Programmer  -   Jeff Wrench                                             */
/*                                                                              */
/*-1*******************************************************************************/
```

```
line_to(x, y)
int x, y;
{

    line ( x - CURx, y - CURy );   /* Just convert to a relative move */
}

/*+1*********************************************************************/
/*                                                                     */
/*      text_bbox   -   sets bounding box for text                     */
/*                                                                     */
/*      description -   sets the bounding box for a text string using the */
/*                      justification given.                           */
/*                                                                     */
/*      parameters  -   text_bbox(string,  jh,  jv)                    */
/*                      char *string;          string to bound         */
/*                      char jh;               horizontal justification */
/*                      char jv;               vertical justification  */
/*                                                                     */
/*      returns     -   a pointer to a bounding box for the text string */
/*                                                                     */
/*      Programmer  -   Jeff Wrench                                    */
/*                                                                     */
/*-1*********************************************************************/

rect_t *text_bbox(string,  jh,  jv)
char *string, jh, jv;
{
int len;
rect_t *retval;

    len = strlen(string) * 8;            /* length in pixels of string */

    retval = inst_rect(0, 0, len, 8);   /* get rectangle for LEFT BOTTOM just */

    switch ( (int) jh )        /* Justify it horizontally */
    {
        case MIDDLE:
                offset_rect ( retval, ( - len ) / 2, 0 );
                break;
        case RIGHT:
                offset_rect ( retval, - len, 0 );
                break;
    }
```

```
    switch ( (int) jv )              /* justify it vertically */
    {
        case TOP:
                    offset_rect ( retval, 0, -8 );
                    break;
        case CENTER:
                    offset_rect ( retval, 0, -4 );
                    break;
    }

    return ( retval );  /* return the bounding box */
}

/*+1*********************************************************************/
/*                                                                    */
/*      draw_text   -   draw a string on the screen                   */
/*                                                                    */
/*      description -   Draws String at ( X, Y ) with justification   */
/*                                                                    */
/*      parameters  -   draw_text(string, x, y, bbox);                */
/*                      char *string;               string to print   */
/*                      int x, y;               where to print the string */
/*                      rect_t *bbox;           justification from text_bbox */
/*                                                                    */
/*      returns     -   nothing                                       */
/*                                                                    */
/*      Programmer  -   Jeff Wrench                                   */
/*                                                                    */
/*-1*********************************************************************/

draw_text(string, x, y, bbox)
char *string;
int x, y;
rect_t *bbox;
{
int chrx, chry;
char *str;

    x += bbox->left;                    /* get upper left of first character */
    y += bbox->top;

    /* map viewable bbox */
    map( &x, &y);    /* map to screen */
```

```
    for ( str = string; *str; str++, x += 8 )    /* print the characters */
        genchr(x, y, *str);
}

/*+1******************************************************************/
/*                                                                   */
/*      fill_rect    -   Fills a rectangle                           */
/*                                                                   */
/*      description -   Fills a rectangle after clipping it to the window */
/*                                                                   */
/*      parameters  -   fill_rect(rect_pointer)                      */
/*                      rect_t *rect_pointer    rectangle to be filled */
/*                                                                   */
/*      returns     -   nothing                                      */
/*                                                                   */
/*      Programmer  -   Jeff Wrench                                  */
/*                                                                   */
/*-1******************************************************************/

fill_rect(rect_pointer)
rect_t *rect_pointer;
{
int i, j;
int savx, savy;
rect_t r;

    savx = CURx;
    savy = CURy;

    if(sect_rect(rect_pointer, cur_win, &r))     /* clip the rectangle */
    {
        for ( i = r.bottom; i <= r.top; i++ )    /* fill one line at a time */
        {
            CURy = i;
            CURx = r.left;
            line_to ( r.right, CURy );
        }
    }
    CURx = savx;
    CURy = savy;
}
```

```
/*+1*******************************************************************/
/*                                                                   */
/*      clear_vport -   clears the current view port                 */
/*                                                                   */
/*      description -   clears the current view_port and redraws the screen */
/*                      rectangle                                    */
/*                                                                   */
/*      parameters  -   clear_vport(vport)                           */
/*                      vport_t *vport;          the view port to be cleared */
/*                                                                   */
/*      returns     -   nothing                                      */
/*                                                                   */
/*      programmer  -   Jeff Wrench                                  */
/*                                                                   */
/*-1*******************************************************************/

clear_vport(vport)
vport_t *vport;
{
int i, j;
char tmpcolor;

    tmpcolor = color;

    i = CURx;
    j = CURy;

    set_color(vport->bkgnd);

    fill_rect ( vport->bitmap );   /* fill the view port with background */

    set_color(vport->brder);

    CURx = vport->bitmap->left;
    CURy = vport->bitmap->top;

    /* draw the border */

    line_to(vport->bitmap->right, vport->bitmap->top);
    line_to(vport->bitmap->right, vport->bitmap->bottom);
    line_to(vport->bitmap->left, vport->bitmap->bottom);
    line_to(vport->bitmap->left, vport->bitmap->top);
```

```
        CURx = i;
        CURy = j;

        color = tmpcolor;
}


/*+1*****************************************************************************/
/*                                                                            */
/*      fill_oval   -   fills an oval                                         */
/*                                                                            */
/*      description -   Fills an oval bounded by rect_pointer.  It calls      */
/*                      frame_oval() to save code                            */
/*                                                                            */
/*      parameters  -   fill_oval ( rect_pointer )                           */
/*                      rect_t *rect_pointer;    bounding box of oval to fill */
/*                                                                            */
/*      returns     -   nothing                                              */
/*                                                                            */
/*      Programmer  -   Jeff Wrench                                          */
/*                                                                            */
/*-1*****************************************************************************/

fill_oval(rect_pointer)
rect_t *rect_pointer;
{
    OVALF = 1;              /* say we're filling */

    frame_oval(rect_pointer);   /* do the fill */

    OVALF = 0;              /* go back to default frame */
}
```

```
/*+1*************************************************************************/
/*                                                                         */
/*      frame_oval    -    frames an oval                                  */
/*                                                                         */
/*      description -    Frames an oval bounded by rect_pointer.           */
/*                                                                         */
/*      parameters  -    fill_oval ( rect_pointer )                        */
/*                       rect_t *rect_pointer;    bounding box of oval to fill */
/*                                                                         */
/*      returns     -    nothing                                          */
/*                                                                         */
/*      Programmer  -    Jeff Wrench                                       */
/*                                                                         */
/*-1*************************************************************************/


frame_oval(rect_pointer)
rect_t *rect_pointer;
{
int x, y, alpha, beta, u, v;
long k;
long k1, k2, k3, a, b;
long d;
int *coord1, *coord2, *coord3, d1, d2, d3;
int w;
int count;
int oldx, oldy;
int xoff, yoff;
int left, right, top, bottom;
int xcent, ycent;
rect_t r;

   if(sect_rect(rect_pointer, cur_win, &r))      /* clip it down if needed */
   {
       map( &(r.left),  &(r.bottom));  /* map to screen */
       map( &(r.right), &(r.top));

       /* xoff is the distance from the left to center of oval */
       xoff = ( ( r.right - r.left ) / 2 ) + r.left;

       /* yoff is the distance from the top to center of oval */
       yoff = ( ( r.bottom - r.top ) / 2 ) + r.top;
```

```
        /*make center relative 0,0 */
        xcent = ycent = 0;

        /* move bounding box so the center is relative at 0,0 */
        offset_rect ( &r, - xoff, - yoff );

        left   = r.left;
        right  = r.right;
        top    = r.top;
        bottom = r.bottom;

/* ellipse is calculated by the formula (x*x)/(a*a) + (y*y)/(b*b) = 1 */
/* so I plug the point above the current into the formula and the point */
/* to the right of the current into the formula and the one closest to 1 */
/* is the next point on the ellipse */

        set_d(&r);    /* set A squared and B squared */

        x = left;
        oldy = y = 0;

        CURx = x + xoff;
        CURy = yoff;

/* draw the first line or first 2 points of the ellipse */

        if ( OVALF )
            hline ( CURx, ( xoff * 2 ) - CURx, CURy );
        else
        {
        int disx, disy;

            disx = 2 * ( xoff - CURx );
            disy = 2 * ( yoff - CURy );
            do_pix();

            CURx += disx;
            do_pix();
        }
```

```
while ( x < 0 )
{
    d1 = do_d (x + 1, y );   /* plug next possible point into formula */
    d2 = do_d (x, y + 1 );

    if ( d1 < d2 )           /* which one is closest */
        x++;
    else
        y++;

    CURx = x + xoff;         /* set next point relative to screen */
    CURy = yoff + y;

    if ( OVALF )
    {
        /* draw the line */
        if ( oldy == y ) continue;
        hline ( CURx, ( xoff * 2 ) - CURx, CURy );
        CURx = x + xoff;
        CURy -= ( abs ( CURy - yoff ) * 2 );
        /* mirror the line around the x-axis */
        hline ( CURx, ( xoff * 2 ) - CURx, CURy );
        oldy = y;
    }
    else
    {
    int disx, disy;

        disx = 2 * ( xoff - CURx );
        disy = 2 * ( yoff - CURy );

        /* plot a point in each quadrant */

        do_pix();

        CURx += disx;
        do_pix();

        CURy += disy;
        do_pix();
```

```
                        CURx -= disx;
                        do_pix();
                }
            }
        }
}


/*****************************************/
/* hline prints a horizontal line  */
/*****************************************/

hline( x1, x2, y )
int x1, x2, y;
{
    CURy = y;
    for ( CURx = x1; CURx <= x2; CURx++ )
        do_pix();
}

static double a, b;
/*********************************************************************/
/* set_d - computes A squared and B squared for the given ellipse */
/*********************************************************************/

static set_d ( r )
rect_t *r;
{
double tmp;

    tmp = (double) ( ( - r->left ) + r->right ) / 2.0;
    a = tmp * tmp;
    tmp = (double) ( ( - r->top ) + r->bottom ) / 2.0;
    b = tmp * tmp;
}
```

```
/*******************************************************************/
/* do_d - plugs the given point into the ellipse form and returns the answer  */
/*******************************************************************/

static double do_d( x, y )
int x, y;
{
    return ( abs ( ( (double) ( x * x ) / a ) + ( (double) ( y * y ) / b ) ) );
}

static int fence;

/*+1***************************************************************/
/*                                                                */
/*      fill_poly    -   fills the polygon                        */
/*                                                                */
/*      description -   fills the given polygon by building a move table of  */
/*                      the polygon, then feeds it into the fill algorithm.  */
/*                      The fill algorithm works by xoring a line from the   */
/*                      bounding box to current point on the polygon.  All   */
/*                      points on the inside are xored an odd number of times */
/*                      so they stay the color while points on the outside are*/
/*                      xored an even number of times so they return to the   */
/*                      original color.                           */
/*                                                                */
/*      parameters   -   fill_poly(poly);                         */
/*                      poly_t *poly;    polygon to be filled      */
/*                                                                */
/*      returns      -   nothing                                  */
/*                                                                */
/*      Programmer   -   Jeff Wrench                              */
/*                                                                */
/*-1***************************************************************/

fill_poly(poly_pointer)
poly_t *poly_pointer;
{
char table[4000], *p = table, move;
int x, y, n, i;

    build_tab(poly_pointer, table);
```

```
    x = poly_pointer->point->point.x;    /* get starting point */
    y = poly_pointer->point->point.y;

    n = 1;

    p = table;

    for ( move = get_move( &n, &p ); move;   /* move until finished with poly */
          move = get_move( &n, &p ) )
    {
        switch ( move )
        {
            case RT:              /* move right */
                    x++;
                    break;
            case LT:              /* move left */
                    x--;
                    break;
            case UP:              /* move up */
                    clr_line( x, y++ );
                    break;
            case DN:              /* move down */
                    clr_line( x, --y );
                    break;
            case UPRT:            /* move up right */
                    clr_line( ++x, y++ );
                    break;
            case UPLT:            /* move up left */
                    clr_line( --x, y++ );
                    break;
            case DNRT:            /* move down right */
                    clr_line( ++x, --y );
                    break;
            case DNLT:            /* move down left */
                    clr_line( --x, --y );
                    break;


        }
    }
}
```

```
/***************************************************/
/* clr_line - xor's a line with the current color */
/***************************************************/

clr_line( x, y )
{
int i;

    for ( i = fence; i < x; i++ )
        xor_pix ( i, y );
}


/*+1*********************************************************************/
/*                                                                     */
/*       build_tab    -    Builds a move table                         */
/*                                                                     */
/*       description  -    Builds a move table                         */
/*                                                                     */
/*       parameters   -    build_table( poly, table );                 */
/*                         poly_t *poly;           poly to build       */
/*                         char   *table;          table to put moves  */
/*                                                                     */
/*       returns      -    nothing                                     */
/*                                                                     */
/*       programmer   -    Jeff Wrench                                 */
/*                                                                     */
/*-1*********************************************************************/

build_tab ( poly, table )
poly_t *poly;
char *table;
{
int x1, x2, y1, y2, n = 1;
int ox1 = -1, ox2 = -1, oy1 = -1, oy2 = -1;
int cd1, cd2, point_in;
char *p;
cpoint_t *np, *sp, *bp, *ep, *lp;

    p = table;
```

```
        /* are there two points on the polygon */
        if ( ( ! poly ) || ( ! poly->point ) || ( ! poly->point->next ) ) /* no */
        {
            table[0] = 0;
            return;
        }


        x2 = poly->point->point.x;   /* get first point */
        y2 = poly->point->point.y;

        fence = x2;

        for ( np = poly->point->next; np; np = np->next )
        {

            x1 = x2;            /* reset first point to old last point */
            y1 = y2;

            x2 = np->point.x;   /* get the new last point */
            y2 = np->point.y;

            do_line(x1, y1, x2, y2, &p, &n);  /* do the line */
        }
        *(++p) = '\0';         /* end table with a null */
}

/*+1*****************************************************************************/
/*                                                                            */
/*      do_line      -   builds a line of moves                               */
/*                                                                            */
/*      description  -   builds a line of moves and puts them in the table    */
/*                       the algorithm is the same as line()                  */
/*                                                                            */
/*      parameters   -   do_line ( x1, y1, x2, x2, p, n )                      */
/*                       int x1, y1;      starting point                      */
/*                       int x2, y2;      ending point                        */
/*                       char **p;        pointer to pointer into the table   */
/*                                                                            */
/*      returns      -   nothing                                              */
/*                                                                            */
/*      Programmer   -   Jeff Wrench                                          */
/*                                                                            */
/*-1*****************************************************************************/
```

```
do_line(x1, y1, x2, y2, p, n)
int x1, y1, x2, y2, *n;
char **p;
{
int xprev, yprev, byts;
int dx, dy, adx, ady, xa, ya, d, incr1, incr2;

    if ( fence > x2 ) fence = x2;

    xprev = x1;
    yprev = y1;

    dx = x2-x1;
    dy = y2-y1;

    if ( dx < 0 )               /* Set up to move backward on the X-axis */
    {
        xa = -1;
        adx = -dx;
    }
    else                        /* Set up to move forward on the X-axis */
    {
        xa =  1;
        adx = dx;
    }

    if ( dy < 0 )               /* Set up to move backward on the Y-axis */
    {
        ya = -1;
        ady = -dy;
    }
    else                        /* Set up to move forward on the Y-axis */
    {
        ya =  1;
        ady = dy;
    }
```

```
if (adx > ady)
{
    incr1 = ady << 1;
    incr2 = (d = incr1 - adx) - adx;

    do
    {
        x1 += xa;
        if (d < 0)
            d += incr1;
        else
        {
            y1 += ya;
            d += incr2;
        }
        **p = do_move(x1-xprev, y1-yprev, **p, n);
        xprev = x1;
        yprev = y1;
        if ( *n )
        {
            *(++(*p)) = '\0' ;
            ++byts;
        }
    } while (x1 != x2);
}
else
{
    incr1 = adx << 1;
    incr2 = (d = incr1 - ady) - ady;

    do
    {
        y1 += ya;
        if (d < 0)
            d += incr1;
        else
        {
            x1 += xa;
            d += incr2;
        }
```

```
            **p = do_move(x1-xprev, y1-yprev, **p, n);
            xprev = x1;
            yprev = y1;
            if ( *n )
            {
                *(++(*p)) = '\0';
                ++byts;
            }
        } while (y1 != y2);
    }
}


/*+1*************************************************************************/
/*                                                                        */
/*      do_move       -   does one pixel move                             */
/*                                                                        */
/*      description  -   does a one pixel move                            */
/*                                                                        */
/*      parameters   -   do_move ( dx, dy, curbyt, n )                    */
/*                       int dx, dy;      direction of move               */
/*                       int curbyt;      the current byte of the table   */
/*                       int *n;          which nibble to put move in     */
/*                                                                        */
/*      returns      -   The new byte for the table                      */
/*                                                                        */
/*      programmer   -   Jeff Wrench                                      */
/*                                                                        */
/*-1*************************************************************************/

do_move(dx, dy, curbyt, n)
int dx, dy, *n, curbyt;
{

unsigned int nibble;

    nibble = 0;

    if (dx)
    {
        if (dx < 0)
            nibble = 0x0c;
        else
            nibble = 0x04;
    }
```

```
    if (dy)
    {
        if (dy < 0)
            nibble |= 0x03;
        else
            nibble |= 0x01;
    }


    /* put the move into the proper nibble */
    nibble = (*n) ? (nibble << 4) : (curbyt  & 0xfff0 ) | nibble;

    if (*n)
        *n = 0;
    else
        *n = 1;

    return (nibble);
}
/*+1*******************************************************************/
/*                                                                   */
/*      get_move    -    gets the next move                          */
/*                                                                   */
/*      description -    gets the next move from the move table      */
/*                                                                   */
/*      parameters  -    get_move ( n, p )                           */
/*                       int *n;    which nibble to use              */
/*                       char **p;  pointer to a pointer into the table */
/*                                                                   */
/*      returns     -    the new move                                */
/*                                                                   */
/*      programmer  -    Jeff Wrench                                 */
/*                                                                   */
/*-1*******************************************************************/

char get_move( n, p )
int *n;
char **p;
{
char *p1, nibble;
```

```
    p1 = *p;

    nibble = *p1;

    if ( *n )                /* get right nibble */
    {
        nibble = ( nibble >> 4 ) & 0x0f;
        *n = 0;
    }
    else
    {
        nibble &= 0x0f;
        *n = 1;
        (*p)++;              /* if last nibble inc to byte of table */
    }


    return (nibble);
}

/*+1***********************************************************************/
/*                                                                       */
/*       do_pix      -   Does a pixel                                    */
/*                                                                       */
/*       description -   Turns the given pixel to the current set_color  */
/*                                                                       */
/*       parameters  -   do_pix ()                                       */
/*                                                                       */
/*       returns     -   Nothing                                         */
/*                                                                       */
/*       Programmer  -   Jeff Wrench                                     */
/*                                                                       */
/*-1***********************************************************************/

do_pix()
{
    if ( CURx & 1 )
        colorb = ( color >> 2 ) & 3;
    else
        colorb = color & 3;
```

```
    reg1.ax = Øxc00 | colorb;
    reg1.cx = CURx;
    reg1.dx = CURy;
    sysint( Øx10, &reg1, &reg2 );
}


/*+1***************************************************************************/
/*                                                                          */
/*      xor_pix     -   Does a pixel                                        */
/*                                                                          */
/*      description -   Turns the given pixel to the current set_color      */
/*                      after clipping the pixel                            */
/*                                                                          */
/*      parameters  -   xor_pix( x, y )                                     */
/*                                                                          */
/*      returns     -   Nothing                                            */
/*                                                                          */
/*      Programmer  -   Jeff Wrench                                        */
/*                                                                          */
/*-1***************************************************************************/

xor_pix( x, y )
int x, y;
{
    if ( clip_code ( x, y, cur_win ) )  /* is pixel in window */
        return;           /* no */

    map ( &x, &y );       /* map to screen */

    if ( x & 1 )
        colorb = ( color >> 2 ) & 3;
    else
        colorb = color & 3;

    reg1.ax = Øxc80 | colorb;
    reg1.cx = x;
    reg1.dx = y;
    sysint( Øx10, &reg1, &reg2 );
}
```

```
/*+1****************************************************************************/
/*                                                                            */
/*      genchr       -    generates a character                               */
/*                                                                            */
/*      description  -    generates a character at the given position, I use  */
/*                        instead of BIOS because I want to start a character */
/*                        anywhere on screen                                  */
/*                                                                            */
/*      parameters   -    genchr( x, y, chr )                                 */
/*                        int x, y;        position of upper left of character */
/*                        char chr;        character to print                 */
/*                                                                            */
/*      returns      -    nothing                                            */
/*                                                                            */
/*      Programmer   -    Jeff Wrench                                         */
/*                                                                            */
/*-1****************************************************************************/

genchr ( x, y, chr )
int x, y;
char chr;
{
unsigned pos, seg;
int i, j;
int chrtodo[8];
int savx, savy;

    savx = CURx;
    savy = CURy;

    if ( chr < 128 )
    {
        pos = (int) chr << 3;    /* mult by 8 because 8 bytes per char */
        pos += 0xfa6e;           /* BIOS character table for first 128 chars */
        seg = 0xf000;
    }
    else
    {
        pos = ( (int) chr - 128 ) << 3; /* mult by 8 because 8 bytes per char */
        pos += peek ( 0x1f * 4, 0 );
        seg = peek ( ( 0x1f * 4 ) + 2, 0 );
    }
```

```
    for ( i = 0; i < 8; i++ )              /* read the char into memory */
        chrtodo[i] = peek ( pos + i, seg ) & 0xff;

    for ( i = 0; i < 8; i++ )              /* eight lines per char of */
        for ( j = 0; j < 8; j++ )          /* eight bits across */
        {
            chrtodo[i] <<= 1;
            if ( chrtodo[i] & 0x100 )       /* is this bit on */
            {                               /* if so turn the pixel on */
                CURx = x + j;
                CURy = y + i;
                do_pix();
            }
        }

    CURx = savx;
    CURy = savy;
}

/*****************************************************/
/* move_to - moves current position to (x, y) */
/*****************************************************/

move_to(x, y)
int     x, y;
{
    CURx = x;
    CURy = y;
}

/****************************************************************/
/* move - moves current position to (x + current, y + current) */
/****************************************************************/

move(x, y)
int     x, y;
{
    CURx += x;
    CURy += y;
}
```

Index

More Computer Knowledge from Que

Que Order Line: **1-800-428-5331**

All prices subject to change without notice.

LEARN MORE ABOUT C
WITH THESE OUTSTANDING BOOKS FROM QUE

C Self-Study Guide
by Jack Purdum

This self-directed study guide uses a unique question-and-answer format to take you through the basics and into advanced areas of the C programming language. The book includes complete programs for testing new functions and for illustrating tips, traps, techniques, and shortcuts. A perfect companion for the *C Programming Guide*, this book will help you teach yourself to program in C. A companion disk is available.

C Programming Guide, 2nd Edition
by Jack Purdum

Keep up-to-date on the latest developments in the C programming language with this revised edition of the best-selling *C Programming Guide*. This popular tutorial shows you the secrets of experts—the tips, tricks, and techniques that take so long to learn on your own. Gain the knowledge and skill you need to venture into all areas of programming, from operating systems to accounting packages, with this highly respected book.

Common C Functions
by Kim J. Brand

This book displays dozens of C functions that are designed to teach C coding techniques to provide useful building blocks for program development. Learn the elements and structures of C programming by studying C code written by others. If you want to gain a stronger understanding of C code and how it works, *Common C Functions* is a superb guide. All the C code in this book is available on disk.

C Programmer's Library
by Jack Purdum, Timothy Leslie, and Alan Stegemoller

The most advanced book about C on the market today, this best-seller will save you hours of programming time and help you write more efficient code. Author Jack Purdum discusses design considerations in writing programs and offers programming tips to help you take full advantage of the power of C. A disk containing all the programs in the book is available.

Item	Title	Price	Quantity	Extension
176	C Self-Study Guide	$ 16.95		
284	Companion Disk, IBM PC format	39.95		
285	Companion Disk, 8-inch SS/SD	39.95		
148	Common C Functions	17.95		
280	Companion Disk, IBM PC format	49.95		
281	Companion Disk, 8-inch SS/SD	49.95		
188	C Programming Guide, 2nd Edition	19.95		
45	C Programmer's Library	19.95		
270	Companion Disk, IBM PC format	124.95		
271	Companion Disk, 8-inch SS/SD	124.95		

Book Subtotal	
Shipping & Handling ($1.75 per item)	
Indiana Residents Add 5% Sales Tax	
GRAND TOTAL	

Method of Payment:

☐ Check ☐ VISA ☐ MasterCard ☐ American Express

Card Number _____ Exp. Date _____

Cardholder Name _____

Ship to _____

Address _____

City _____ State _____ ZIP _____

If you can't wait, call **1-800-428-5331** and order TODAY.

All prices subject to change without notice.

AC-859

REGISTRATION CARD

Register your copy of *Advanced C: Techniques & Applications* and receive the latest issue of */c: The Journal for C Users*—FREE. Just complete this registration card and return it to Que Corporation. You also will receive information about Que's newest products relating to the C programming language and the UNIX operating system.

Name _____

Address _____

City _____ State _____ ZIP _____

Phone _____

Where did you buy your copy of *Advanced C*?

_____

How do you plan to use the programs in this book?

_____

_____

What other kinds of publications about C and UNIX would you be interested in?

_____

Which C compiler do you use? _____

Version number _____

Which operating system do you use? _____

Which computer? _____

THANK YOU!

AC-859